PEOPLES OF
THE GRAN CHACO

Also Available in
Native Peoples of the Americas

The Archaeological Northeast
Mary Ann Levine, Kenneth E. Sassaman, and Michael S. Nassaney, editors

PEOPLES OF THE GRAN CHACO

Edited by
Elmer S. Miller

Native Peoples of the Americas
Laurie Weinstein, General Editor

BERGIN & GARVEY
Westport, Connecticut • London

Library of Congress Cataloging-in-Publication Data

Peoples of the Gran Chaco / edited by Elmer S. Miller.
     p.   cm.—(Native peoples of the Americas, ISSN 1521–5091)
   Includes bibliographical references and index.
   ISBN 0–89789–532–0 (alk. paper)
   1. Indians of South America—Gran Chaco. I. Miller, Elmer S.,
  1931– . II. Series.
  F2821.1.C47P46   1999
  982′.300498—dc21   98–41385

British Library Cataloguing in Publication Data is available.

Library of Congress Catalog Card Number: 98–41385
ISBN: 0–89789–532–0
ISSN: 1521–5091

First published in 1999

Bergin & Garvey, 88 Post Road West, Westport, CT 06881
An imprint of Greenwood Publishing Group, Inc.
www.greenwood.com

Printed in the United States of America

The paper used in this book complies with the
Permanent Paper Standard issued by the National
Information Standards Organization (Z39.48–1984).

10 9 8 7 6 5 4 3 2 1

Contents

Illustrations

MAPS

PHOTOGRAPHS

Series Foreword

Laurie Weinstein

Peoples of the Gran Chaco, edited by Elmer Miller, is one of the first books in Bergin and Garvey's new series The Native Peoples of the Americas. This multivolume series will cover indigenous peoples in North, Middle, and South America. Each volume will explore the history and cultural survival of native peoples by telling a unique story. Some volumes will focus on competing ethnicities and the struggle for resources. Other volumes will illuminate the archaeology and ethnohistory of particular regions. Still other volumes will explore gender relations, warfare, and native cosmologies and ethnobotanies. Yet, despite the particular foci or theoretical frameworks of the editor and his or her contributors, all volumes will reveal the rich cultural tapestry of the American continents. Together, these volumes will chronicle a common historical theme: despite the invasion of foreign explorers, traders, militia, missionaries, and colonists beginning in the sixteenth century, despite rapid native depopulation due to disease and overt Anglo policies of ethnocide, despite the penetration of a capitalistic market system into tribal economies, native peoples have survived. As this volume and subsequent volumes will illustrate, native peoples are learning how to organize politically and economically; they know that their values, languages, oral traditions, and other aspects of culture are worth preserving.

Elmer Miller's fascinating anthology about the Gran Chaco of South America brings together a variety of scholars who describe life among the 'Weenhayek, the Enxet, the Guaraní, and the Eastern and Western Toba. These groups constitute native populations of present-day Argentina, Bolivia, and Paraguay. Jan-Åke Alvarsson describes what it is like as an anthropologist to live with the 'Weenhayek of Bolivia and Argentina. He goes on a hunt and, much to the dismay of the 'Weenhayek, urges them to release a captured armadillo. Stephen Kidd draws readers into the lives of the Enxet, who still follow their traditional mores of generosity and reciprocity despite the materialistic trappings of modern Paraguayans. They give or loan everything away.

Silvia María Hirsch describes her impressions of the *capitanía*, the political arm of the Guaraní of eastern Bolivia. This new political body of traditional chiefs has been successfully used to negotiate conflicts with white ranchers and nongovernmental organizations (NGOs). The Western Toba, studied by Marcela Mendoza, enjoy a "good fight" between women, and the whole village may turn out to watch. Much of the fighting among the Toba, especially between men, is ritualized. Little physical harm is actually incurred, but the incident that prompted the "fight" is usually settled.

While it may be difficult for us to envision South American Indians practicing Pentecostalism, Elmer Miller relates the success of this movement among the Eastern Toba of Argentina. He uses native testimonies to show this people's novel incorporation of a foreign religion into traditional culture. Pablo Wright tells the story of Indian urban migration through the eyes of Valentín Moreno, a Toba man. We learn not only about his search for meaningful work but also about his search for his own Indian identity. It is fitting that this volume end with Moreno's story, which symbolizes the struggle for ethnic survival and the persistence of "Indianness" in the Americas.

Laurie Weinstein
General Editor
Native Peoples of the Americas

Preface

Elmer S. Miller

The Gran Chaco region of South America provides an excellent setting for investigating the impact of nation-state policies upon indigenous populations. Consider the following: (1) the region remained isolated throughout the colonial period and into the twentieth century, even after the nation-states of Argentina, Paraguay, and Bolivia had been established; (2) despite significant variation in language groups with dialectal subdivisions, a hunting, collecting, and fishing economy was common throughout; (3) band-type families adapted to different ecological niches in unique ways, yet shared common sociocultural features everywhere; (4) each nation developed its own political economy with unique policies for conquering and controlling indigenous territory, as well as for incorporating the various native populations into a national work force.

Yet the Chaco remains an enigma to the average North American reader. While the region is commonly recognized as the "Green Hell," little is known about it or its people. This work intends to change that. Seven scholars write here about indigenous life in the three distinct nations. José Braunstein and Elmer S. Miller sketch an overview that provides historical and contemporary context for interpreting the chapters that follow.

Jan-Åke Alvarsson's chapter on the Bolivian 'Weenhayek (known in the literature as Mataco; other Argentine Mataco groups are now identified as Wichí) recounts his own interactions with a foraging people who are currently experiencing dramatic changes in lifestyle. Stephen W. Kidd shows how the Paraguayan Enxet (known in the early literature as Lengua) draw upon their own moral principles to pursue political-economic goals they value, but which increasingly conflict with governmental and NGO projects designed to assimilate them into the nation-state. Silvia María Hirsch describes the actions that have enabled a group of Paraguayan Guaraní to maintain a significant degree of political autonomy despite similar pressures to assimilate.

The last three chapters focus on the Toba, whose various groupings have constituted the largest and most visible indigenous populations in the Argentine Chaco. Marcela Mendoza describes subsistence practices, gender relations, and aggression among the Western Toba, who have remained independent of eastern groups throughout both colonial and national history. Elmer Miller stresses a growing ethnic awareness and commitment among scattered settlements of Eastern Toba, concentrating on the role of the religious *culto* movement in promoting interactions across group boundaries. Pablo G. Wright's account of an individual Toba man who has made Buenos Aires his major residence during the past fifty years provides keen insight into the urbanization processes that increasingly confront all indigenous Chaco families. While each author places emphasis on a particular aspect of social life (environmental values, moral economy, political action, subsistence and gender relations, religious beliefs and actions, on jobs in the city), the reader will be struck by similarities in the values shared by all peoples concerned, as well as by the common problems they confront in their efforts to resist full absorption into the nation-states where their values and sense of unique identity are threatened.

I wish to express my sincere appreciation to Mario and Marcela Mendoza for constructing maps 1 and 2, to Murial Kirkpatrick for map 9, to Charles Eberline for his superb job of copyediting, and finally, to each contributing author who had to put up with my impatient critiques.

PEOPLES OF
THE GRAN CHACO

1

❈ ❈ ───── ❈ ❈

Ethnohistorical Introduction

José Braunstein and
Elmer S. Miller

Since pre-Columbian times, the Gran Chaco has been inhabited by peoples characterized by a nomadic or seminomadic economy (which they largely still preserve) based upon hunting, fishing, gathering, and seasonal horticulture. After the arrival of Europeans in the Americas, the area became a sanctuary for its indigenous inhabitants, as well as for other Amerindian groups escaping from colonial pressure on the periphery. However, with the penetration of nonindigenous settlers from the early decades of this century and the territorial control exercised by the nation-states claiming jurisdiction over the region, most indigenous inhabitants have become increasingly sedentarized.[1]

According to current linguistic knowledge, eighteen surviving languages are spoken by an estimated indigenous population of some 260,000 people, classified into six linguistic families: (1) Mataco-Mataguayo, including Wichí/'Weenhayek (Mataco), Nivaklé (Chulupí), Manjuy (Chorote), and Maká; (2) Guaycurú, comprising Toba, Pilagá, Mocoví, and Mbayá;[2] (3) Maskoy, consisting of Enxet (Lengua), Sanapaná, Angaité, Enenxet (Toba-Maskoy), and Kaskiha; (4) Zamuco, involving Chamacoco and Ayoreo; (5) Lule-Vilela, consisting of only a few remaining Vilela (Chunupí); and (6) Tupí Guaraní, comprised of Chiriguano, also known as Guaraní-Guarayo, and Tapieté, also called Guaraní-Ñandeva. (See map 1.)

PHYSICAL GEOGRAPHY AND ECOLOGICAL CONSTRAINTS

The Gran Chaco constitutes a great plain spanning parts of Argentina, Bolivia, and Paraguay. Bounded on the west by the Andean foothills, to the south by the Salado River basin, on the east by the Paraguay and Paraná

Map 1. Gran Chaco Region with Societal Locations

rivers, and on the north by the Mato Grosso plateau, it covers a lowland area of over 600,000 square kilometers. As a result of geological movements that the Brazilian shield underwent in the Tertiary period, the region was inundated until the Pliocene, when the land rose and the sea retreated, leaving a deposit of continental sediment. This layer of mud and clay, which reaches a depth of up to 3,000 meters, explains the almost total absence of stones in the Chaco, a feature that has marked the technology of its indigenous inhabitants, whose sharp instruments were made of hardwoods, bone, or imported raw materials.

Topographically, the main feature of the region is a combination of low elevations and shallow depressions in which streams, lagoons, and wetlands form. The surface of the land declines in a southeasterly direction from the Andean foothills to the Paraguay and Paraná rivers, but the low degree of decline leads to frequent changes of course in the arterial rivers that drain the region: Parapetí, Pilcomayo, Bermejo, and Salado. This fluvial instability gives rise to a proliferation of dry riverbeds that point to a wetter climate and richer hydrological system in the historic past. The wetlands, where beds of clay allow water to collect, generally dry out during the dry season, with isolated lagoons remaining only in the deepest depressions.

Water is the hallmark of the Chaco, due either to its lavish and unruly presence or its oppressive absence. Almost nonexistent precipitation in winter and spring is followed by summer downpours between October and April that account for the region's average annual rainfall of 900 millimeters. The rivers burst their banks, change course, and fill the channels left from previous years, whose millennial fluvial deposits are converted into quagmires. Rainfall is highest in the east, where it reaches up to 1,200 millimeters in summer; it decreases in the west to a maximum of 600 millimeters, but increases again in the shadow of the Andean foothills. (See map 2.)

The lay of the land has a significant influence on the climate inasmuch as it allows for the unimpeded flow of air currents, with cold winds from the south periodically displacing the warm and dusty winds from the north and northeast. Summer temperatures reach well over 40 degrees Celsius, with considerable daily variation, increasing toward the west; there are occasional frosts in the dry season, which help explain the widespread theme of the destruction of the world by frost in Chaco mythology, often interpreted as indicating immigration from the south.

Chaco vegetation before colonization has been described as having consisted of parkland comprising a patchwork of low forests and grasslands, with stands of palm trees in the lower-lying and wetter eastern zone. The aridity of the western and southwestern zones is reflected in the landscape, which includes cacti and thorny leguminous species. Unlike other regions on the same latitude, where similar ecological conditions prevail, the Chaco has not been transformed into a desert of dunes, although some are found in western Paraguay. This is due largely to the hardwood trees that predominate in the forested areas. The resilience of these slow-growing species,

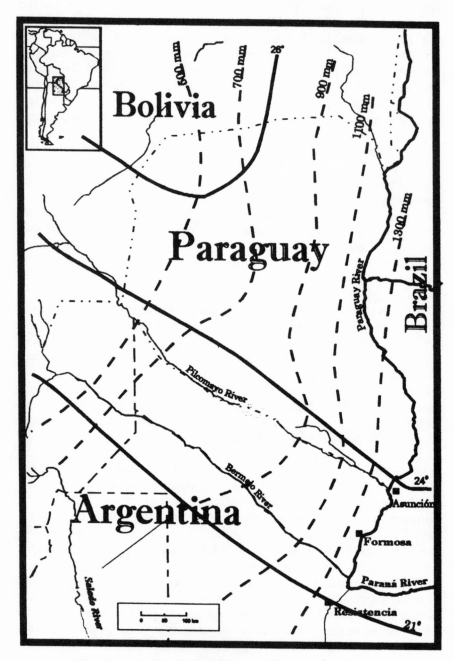

Map 2. Variations in Regional Rainfall and Temperatures

which by the same token makes them almost impossible to reforest, permits the storing of humidity and the stability of the soil over large areas, thereby creating environmental conditions suitable for human and animal life.

The principal floral species found are the *algarrobos* (*Prosopis* sp.), the *quebrachos* (*Schinopsis* sp., *Aspidosperma* sp.), *guayacán* (*Caesalpinía paraguariensis*), which grows to a height of over twenty meters, *mistol* (*Zyzyphus mistol*), *chañar* (*Geoffroea decorticans*), *palo santo* (*Bulnesia sarmientoi*), the bottle tree (*Chorisia insignis*), and various acacias and *Capparis* species. Profusions of epiphytes, cacti (*Cereus* sp.), and *vinal* shoots (*Prosopis ruscifolia*) grow beneath the forest canopy.[3]

A wide range of fauna have formed an important part of the indigenous economies, including carnivores, edentates, members of the Cervidae and Myrmecophagous families, and a variety of rodents and marsupials. The most prominent species include the tapir, the jaguar, the puma and other smaller felines, three types of peccary, several species of deer and armadillo, the anteater, the sloth, and the *aguará guazú* (*Chrysocyon brachiurus*). Among the region's abundant avifauna, the rhea (*Rhea americana*), hunted by means of a camouflage of twigs and leaves, was prized for its meat. The guan (*Cracidae* sp.) also made a substantial contribution to indigenous diets, as do various members of the Tinamidae, Anatidae, and Columbidae families.

SUBSISTENCE PRACTICES

The Gran Chaco peoples have been hunter-gatherers, in contrast to their agriculturalist neighbors on the western border. To speak, though, of hunting is to allude to a wide range of activities, including fishing and the collection of honey, that often made a more significant contribution to the indigenous diet than game animals. Moreover, indigenous languages of the region tend to make little conceptual distinction between the productive and extractive activities or between those of men and women, all of which can be denoted by a single term. Many Chaco groups also have kept a varying number of sheep, goats, and cattle throughout the centuries of contact with Europeans.

Female gathering has played a major role in Chaco economies, complementing the almost exclusively male activities of hunting, fishing, and honey collecting. Throughout the year, groups of related women of different ages made daily incursions into the surrounding area, with their small children, in order to collect produce for their gathering bags; they also collected firewood. A wide variety of products were exploited according to the area and the season: wild fruits, pods, roots, tubers, shoots, palm hearts, bromeliad hearts, and also small animals, fish, and insects. Nowadays, women within reach of towns alternate their gathering in the hinterland with collective forays into the urban environment to gather goods from the nonindigenous sector, which interprets the practice as begging.

Gathering was aimed mainly at food production, but it had other domestic purposes as well, such as provision for traditional medicines and dyes. Of particular importance were the bromeliads, gathered for use both as food and as raw material for string production. Throughout the area, the spinning and weaving of *chaguar* fiber replaced basketry in the production of carrying equipment, such as female gathering bags, male hunting bags and fishing nets, small pouches, and infant slings. It was also the basis for several articles of traditional clothing, while the cat's-cradle games played by all the Chaco peoples were another artifact deriving from this fundamental aspect of their material culture. A characteristically female activity girls practiced during their initiation was cord spinning, inseparably associated with womanhood in most Chaco mythologies.

Various hunting techniques were employed by the men, such as the bow and arrow, fire circles, and different types of traps. The bow was simple and was made of hardwood (usually *Prosopis kuntzei*); arrow shafts were fashioned from reeds, *caña de Castilla* (*Arundo donax*), or a shrub known as *suncho*; they often contained feathers at the rear of the shaft. Projectile points were originally wooden, leaf shaped or serrated, but more recently were made of iron. In winter, when rivers remain in their banks, there is a great abundance of fish, a resource the river people fully exploited. Men caught large specimens, such as shad (*Prochilodus platensis*), *surubí* (*Pseudoplatysoma coruscans*), ox-eyed cackerel (*Leporinus obtusidens*), *bagre* (*Pimelodus* sp.), *pacú* (*Colossoma mitrei*), dorado (*Salminus maxillosus*), and eels. For these species, net fishing was standard, along with the dam or barrage method. In marshes and lagoons, bows and arrows or harpoons were preferred. Techniques employing fishing baskets and vegetable baits were also known. Catching fish by plunging with a net bag (*red de bolsa*) when the water was coldest was also a technique followed by almost all groups. Fish were clobbered to death on the head and then strung through the eyes with a wooden needle for transport. In the Chaco area, crafts such as the dugout canoe made from bottle-tree wood in the middle and lower Pilcomayo and the *pelota* boat made from hides were seldom used for fishing purposes, but rather for fording. Honey produced by different types of bees (*Melipona*) and wasps remains a highly valued staple.

The rainy season constituted for the Chaco peoples the period of large food supplies. Actually, it is not the best fishing time because the largest catches are obtained from low water levels when swamps shrink or rivers subside, but it is the time of blooming forests and ripened fruit, when gathering and cultivation provide abundant yields. Hunting was generally carried out in flooded grounds. Frequent changes in habitat, plus shortages of resources, determined the nomadic life of the Chaco families who roamed constantly and cyclically within fixed territories, seeking the most advantageous conditions. During winter, the scarcity of vegetable supplies made them rely more heavily on fishing or hunting produce. Having no ready access to the waterways, territorial groups of inland people broke up into units that varied in size depending on the availability of resources. With the rains, life became more stable.

In the summer, bands remained in more or less fixed places, a time when older people began to cultivate their gardens. The agriculture was very rudimentary; harvests resembled the picking of wild plants. Among the main implements were the digging stick or the paddlelike leaf-bladed spade. The first cultigens included tobacco, gourds such as squash and pumpkins, beans, manioc, and sweet potatoes. Gourds were used as containers for varied purposes, such as holding liquids, keeping personal belongings, in which case a star-shaped top was cut out, or making rattles filled with seeds. Rattles were the favorite accompaniment to the individual male voice during shaman seances or dances, common in periods involving social concentration. Except for this instrument, which as a rule was not ornamented, other gourds were pyroengraved or incised with geometric or naturalistic motifs. Drinking feasts were frequently held at this time of year, when different types of beer were prepared by fermenting fruits from various kinds of wild plants, especially the *algarroba* bean (*Prosopis*), and frequently with the addition of honey. The ornithological representation of primeval mankind is a recurrent element in mythology, which demonstrates the significance given to birds by Chaco peoples.

EUROPEAN CONTACT

Written references to the Chaco Indians begin with the work of Ulderico Schmidel, a Bavarian soldier on an expedition with Pedro de Mendoza, the first *adelantado* (governor) of La Plata River (see Schmidel 1534–54). Dating back to the 1530s, the information he provides is imprecise, and the identity of the numerous peoples he mentions is a matter of speculation. Another chronicler, the Spanish officer Ruí Díaz de Guzman, made equally confusing references to peoples of the Chaco, although he did identify the Payaguá (on the western bank of the Paraguay River) and the Mbayá-Guaycurú, who were the victims of punitive expeditions led by his uncle, *Adelantado* Alvar Nuñez Cabeza de Vaca. Vague references to people who can with some degree of probability be identified with the present-day indigenous inhabitants of the Gran Chaco first appeared near 1540 when Diego de Rojas, one of Francisco Pizarro's officers, led an expedition southward from Peru. The Jurí who attacked his soldiers are reminiscent of the Surí, whose name (meaning *rhea* in Quechua) is the Quechua equivalent of that given to the Guaycurúan peoples by members of the Mataguayan linguistic family.

In 1585 the first township in the Chaco, Nuestra Señora de la Concepción de la Buena Esperanza, was founded by the order of the last *adelantado* of the La Plata River, Juan de Torres de Vera y Aragón. Established on the south bank of the Bermejo River, the settlement was designed to improve communication between the frontier towns in the west and those built on the major rivers in the east. However, under pressure from indigenous people, who by this time had adopted horses and resisted subjugation to the colonial *encomienda* (estates) system, Concepción was abandoned in 1632.[4]

For the remainder of the seventeenth century, the Chaco peoples successfully resisted Spanish penetration of their lands, which became an asylum for peripheral groups exposed to the full force of the colonial campaign. In the east, the banks of the Paraguay River hosted a steady stream of Amerindians opposed to cultural change, but their advance was limited by the river itself as much as by defensive measures taken by the inhabitants of the colonial city of Asunción. At this time, the Mbayá invaded eastern Paraguay and remained there for approximately 150 years.[5] To the south and west, in contrast, the frontier consisted of a chain of forts and missions protecting the fertile piedmont-type valleys. Its southern extension along the Salado River, where sub-Andean maize cultivators had been living at the time of the Spaniards' arrival, was a semipermeable frontier, and it was here that the slow occupation of the Chaco by whites or, better stated, criollo-pastoralists began.

At the beginning of the eighteenth century, two European currents of thought reached the Spanish colonies that were to create a lasting dichotomy in local politics. The division between medievalist and Enlightenment thinking was exemplified in the policies of successive governors of the colonial province of Tucumán in respect to the frontier. The conservative, militarist position was illustrated by Urizar de Arespacochaga, who in 1710 led an army into the Andean foothills and drove the indigenous communities eastwards. The Enlightenment stance, allied with the Catholic missionary endeavor, which since the Counter-Reformation had been headed by the Society of Jesus, was represented by Governor Gerónimo Matorras. In 1774 the latter led a powerful but peaceful expedition into the Chaco with the aim of subjugating the indigenous population to mission life. The main results of his campaign were a peace treaty with Paiquín, a Mocoví chief who, judging by the chronicles, was one of the most important and ingenious leaders in the Chaco at the time, and the founding of two Franciscan missions among the Toba and Mocoví, San Bernardo and Nuestra Señora de los Milagros de Lacangayé, respectively. The Jesuits had previously established a number of frontier missions, but they had mostly been short-lived, and those that were still in existence at the time of the order's expulsion in 1767 either disappeared or came under the jurisdiction of other religious or lay orders, losing much of their heritage and influence in the process. They included missions among the Mataco in the Bermejo headwaters, among the Lule and Vilela on the Salado, among the Abipón and Mocoví on the Paraná, among the Enimagá and Enxet in the area of present-day Villa Hayes on the west bank of the Paraguay, north of Asunción, and among the Zamuco in Chiquitaña.

As the independence movement gathered momentum, the indigenous question was temporarily overlooked. Enlightenment ideas, and with them the stereotypical image of the Amerindian as natural man, were initially well represented, but the more conservative ideas of the local aristocracy soon prevailed. This ideological shift is reflected in the changing fortunes of the indigenous peoples after independence, in the struggle for which a number of them had participated. To begin with, during the period of civil war when the nation-state was being defined, the policy of treaties and missions was resumed. Subsequently, though, the aboriginal population was of interest on two very different and mutually contradictory accounts. On the one hand, it was seen as a territorial obstruction requiring elimination; on the other, as an unskilled labor force. The former of these two points of view gave rise to the notion of the "desert" in nineteenth-century Argentina, an ethnocentric metaphor for a space that had not been brought under the control of the rule of "law" and "progress."

MIGRATIONS AND CULTURE CHANGE

The complex question of cultural change in the colonial period can be approached from two angles. On the one hand, the adoption of any of a number of colonial cultural elements, from the *mate* beverage and tinderbox to the horse, domestic livestock, and steel, profoundly modified indigenous cultures in the region, initiating, for some groups more than others, a transition from nomadic hunting and gathering to more sedentary forms of subsistence. On the other hand, external pressure resulted in a series of loans and exchanges among the indigenous peoples, converting the Chaco into a cultural melting pot. The hunter-gatherers, for example, both influenced and were influenced by the neighboring agriculturalists, like the sub-Andean Arawak and Lule-Vilela or the Amazonian Guaraní, who had been migrating into the Andean foothills since at least the late fifteenth century.

This account of Chaco peoples departs from the traditional tripartite division into foot people, horse and canoe people, and agriculturalists, stressing instead the flexibility of hunter-gatherer sociopolitical organization over time. In particular, the peripheral groups and those that adopted the horse as a significant cultural element have undergone changes that continue to the present day. The Payaguá of the Paraguay River, for example, were traditionally canoeists who based their economy on water-borne raiding, but when this lifestyle became inviable due to Spanish control, they adapted their nautical technology to a new system of relations with former adversaries based on trade and porterage. A similar picture emerges among the equestrian peoples, whose skillful use of the horse for purposes of war and transportation prevented Spanish penetration of the Chaco until at least the end of the seventeenth century (Schindler 1985). With the subsequent strengthening of the Spanish frontier, they adapted their equestrian mobility to a system of raid and trade, attacking the frontier at one point and exchanging the spoils at another.

The genetic and cultural blending provoked by external pressure on the peripheral societies, particularly along the Salado River frontier, helps to explain one of the enigmas of the historical ethnography of the Chaco. The disappearance of certain ethnic groups mentioned in early chronicles and the later appearance of other previously unknown groups, mysteries that research has thus far failed to explain, can be understood as the product of cultural contact among hunter-gatherer societies forced to share a limited space. With the absence of physical obstacles to communication facilitating internal population movements, moreover, a dynamic process of ethnogenetic symbiosis occurred and continues to occur, leading to communities of mixed cultural and linguistic origin. Under certain circumstances, the degree of intermingling would be intensified, for example, as a result of the ethnic alliances that led to the destruction of Concepción or the displacements caused by military campaigns in the first half of the eighteenth century. The mid-seventeenth-century Calchaquís of the eastern Chaco appear to have consisted of a number of heterogeneous peoples who were forced together, and who developed a unified cultural system with a common pidgin language. Late-eighteenth-century evidence of linguistic stabilization following this process of pidginization suggests the diverse origins of most of the languages spoken in the Chaco today.

SOCIAL ORGANIZATION

The basic unit of social organization in the Chaco has been the "band," a local group of extended families constituted primarily on the basis of kinship and affinity. At an intermediate level of the social system, the "tribe" constituted a regional group of bands often identified by a common name and associated by marriage and exchange (Braunstein 1983:31–35). A tribe was preferentially endogamous, and postmarital residence tended to be uxorilocal, at least initially until the first child was born.[6]

Monogamy continues to be the norm, but polygamous unions are known in some tribes, particularly among band leaders. Marriages tended to be governed by proscriptive rather than prescriptive rules. In general, all members of the bilateral extended family were proscribed, but there was considerable variation. Among certain Mataco tribes, for instance, the proscription covered only members of the nuclear family; Zamuco groups practiced patrilineal sib exogamy, superimposed on a system of local exogamy; the Tupi and Arawak speakers have developed a system that combines both Chaco and Amazonian elements (Braunstein 1983:81–96).

The component bands of a tribe lived in close proximity to one another, with intermittent periods of coresidence, above all in summer at the time of female initiation, for example. The political unity of the tribe depended on the nature of the network of alliances between bands, families, and individuals. In contrast, there was little cohesion at the level of ethnicity involving the collectivity of tribes (each with its own dialect) speaking a common language.[7] But interactions between bands belonging to different linguistic groups were quite common, and, once stabilized, the interethnic units formed of such alliances were the origin of mixed languages and cultures. By exercising political control over access to hunting and fishing grounds, the resulting network of cooperation and antipathy defined the system of land use, although the monopolization of a resource such as barrage fishing, for example, which obstructs the movement of fish along a river, inevitably generated conflict, even between tribal bands.

Leadership was nonauthoritarian, having mainly to do with maintaining the cohesion of the group in terms of both its internal and external relations. Leaders were acknowledged by consensus on the basis of their courage and oratorical skills, although many band leaders were also shamans with inherited curing power (see Miller 1977). Unresolved group hostilities formerly ended in warfare, which typically consisted of a surprise raid in which enemy scalps were taken as trophies. After the hostilities, a drinking feast was held in which the victorious warriors recounted their triumphs and, in certain groups, celebrated with ludic dances in which the scalps of the dead enemies were exhibited. In such cases, the ceremony provided a context in which the system of ranking among war leaders was acknowledged. Intergroup relations were thus marked by two ritual limits: the initiation ceremonies involving social concentration, with, among other things, dances and gift exchanges; or warfare, which also involved collective ceremonies with material and genetic exchange (via the capture of women and children and the appropriation of other valuables). At an intermediate level, the native American hockey and a local form of gambling played between members of allied groups gave expression to those alliances in terms of a symbolic idiom of warfare. Implicitly, they were warlike confrontations that often ended in fighting or, on the contrary, established peace in situations of political tension.

GRAN CHACO PEOPLES IN HISTORICAL CONTEXT

In writing the history of an indigenous region such as the Chaco, it is important to distinguish two different historical perspectives: our own, which anthropologists are wont to call "ethnohistory," and that of the peoples themselves, which will here be called "ethnic history." These two perspectives are often opposed to one another. From a theoretical point of view, ethnicity is dynamic, yet it has no independent reality as far as individual members are concerned. One person can call upon different ethnicities at different times, depending on context and circumstantial strategy. Yet whenever an ethnic identity is mentally construed, it can only be done so in social terms. The construction must necessarily be a historical one, since the various ethnicities are merely expressions of a common traditional ethnic history that an individual shares with others. It is from this standpoint that we say that each subgroup (band or regional group) in the Chaco constitutes a distinct social unit, because each one has a history in mind that differs from those of other groups that conceptualize a different history. Such groups tend to be differentiated most readily by outside investigators on the basis of language.

There is an intentional process of assimilation in South American countries, especially in Argentina, that aims to teach "national history" as a condition of nationality. This colonialist process constitutes ethnocide because it obliterates the different local histories, which are sometime at total variance with what we learn about them, particularly when the same event is portrayed from two different perspectives. A clear example is the history of Gran Chaco occupation by nation-states. There is also another historical distortion imposed by whites that frequently causes a loss of ethnic ownership. It is ideologically in disagreement with the former, but has the same effect and is characteristic of many indigenist organizations. These organizations formulate their own notions about indigenous group identities with their particular histories.

In fact, each adult individual currently living in a community in the Chaco area knows the names and feats of his or her elders, including the various mythic occurrences that in many cases have lost their "presence" in the sense that they no longer constitute a concrete reality connected to life as experienced on a daily basis. The recording of these narratives is deemed imperative now that many Chaco Indian languages are beginning to have their own written form. This is the only way to ensure that the indigenous peoples maintain their individuality as groups, with a definitive culture of their own.

In the past century, when Argentina, Bolivia, and Paraguay adopted their present status of independence from Spain, most of the Gran Chaco was not yet occupied by white people. In fact, the area lies at the heart of the three newborn nation-states. The northern Chaco was occupied militarily by both Bolivians and Paraguayans prior to the Chaco War between Bolivia and Paraguay (1932–35). Large ranches had also been staked out and claimed, including land made available to Mennonite immigrants who arrived in 1927. The relatively peaceful nature of the northern Chaco occupation, in which the Anglican missions played a seminal role, contrasts with that of the southern Chaco. However, the entire Chaco region was devastated by European diseases that produced major depopulation.

Only when the civil wars were over and the constitution of the country was definitively established in 1864 did the Argentine army conduct a systematic occupation of Indian land. At that time, the Argentine government launched an aggressive policy of expansion over the territories claimed by all the neighboring nation-states. The army's action had been previously concentrated on the southern border because for centuries Indian raids had been a nightmare for the rich countryside around Buenos Aires. Later on, in 1884, that action was extended to the Chaco region with the campaign led by the minister of war, General Benjamín Victorica. Several powerful troops of soldiers, arriving from different points, converged on a strategic site where the Teuco River meets the Bermejo. The troops swept the region in a most violent and frightening manner and succeeded in ridding the southern Chaco of Indians, with just a band left on the right bank of the Bermejo; a few others managed to cross the river and head northeast to finally settle in the central Chaco. In 1897, once the 1890 economic crisis had been overcome and the frontier line on the Bermejo had been strengthened, an army division was set up under General Lorenzo Winter, who in the ensuing four years carried out a "pacification" campaign that involved the construction of new outposts and the surrender of the last Indian stronghold south of the Bermejo. Also, following the death of the Spanish explorer Enrique Ibarreta in 1898, a series of harsh punitive expeditions was conducted in the central Chaco that gradually undermined Indian fighting capacity. During these raids, the soldiers attacked Indian villages along their way, burning homes and killing anyone who dared to resist; in this way, they were able to disrupt the political organization of most of the groups in the area by exterminating their main warrior leaders.

In the second decade of the twentieth century, following the law that established compulsory military service and some organizational changes, the army was able to set up new forts in the central Chaco that provided support for the recently created Borders Committee, charged with marking the Paraguay-Argentina frontier after the award of President H. R. Hayes. In those days, the army had plans for a "peaceful conquest of the Indians along with their territory." In 1911 Col. Enrique Rostagno led a military campaign that consolidated the occupation of Indian lands south of the Pilcomayo and founded a number of villages that later developed into some of today's cities. Friction and clashes between Indians and whites were frequent at the time, and the line's cavalry division was there to put them down. Some of the documented cases concern the appearance of salvation religious movements among the Indians (Bartolomé 1972), and others concern raids that, when not commanded by white bandits, may be understood as a way of resistance. In any case, the fierce quarrels between Indians and whites began to steadily decrease over that period until they were reduced to some sporadic border skirmishes. A few Indians established relations with the whites and reached alliances with the military men to fight for territorial control against their long-standing enemies. The Nivaclé were pushed out of their territories south of the Pilcomayo by the Pilagá, who were allied with the army up to 1919, when they were erroneously blamed for the attack on Fort Yunka.

MISSIONIZATION

From the early days of conquest, the Christian religion in various denominational forms played a key role in fomenting processes of change and assimilation of Chaco Indians into Western culture. Until the Jesuits were expelled from the New World in 1767, their missions introduced people not only to God, but to sedentary subsistence practices involving agriculture and a work ethic. In the last hundred years, missionaries from various Christian creeds established instructional relationships with the Chaco Indians; these were primarily Catholic, Anglican, and evangelical of one type or another.

The Catholic presence was in a way a continuation of the missionary activity that had never been altogether interrupted since the initial arrival of the Spaniards. The Chaco missionaries were Franciscans belonging to two different colleges: the Tarija group which preached in the western zone among the Chiriguano of the Bolivian piedmont and the Mataco of the Bermejo basin, and the San Lorenzo group, which worked in the eastern missions of Laishí and Tacaaglé among the Eastern Toba. In Argentina, the 1864 Constitution explicitly stated that Indians should be converted to Catholicism, the institution primarily responsible for their care. Yet the missions did not always have governmental support; often they had serious trouble with the local authorities, mostly because they acted in defense of the abused Indians. Furthermore, a serious lack of personnel and resources resulted in little or no contact with the majority of indigenous Chaco peoples.

Toward the end of the century, several Anglican missions were established, first in Tierra del Fuego and later in the Paraguayan Chaco, where Adolfo Henriksen initiated the work in 1888. Upon his death, W. Barbrooke Grubb took over the Makthlawaiya Mission to the Enxet in 1907 and gave it its main impetus, establishing many mission stations inland from the Paraguay River. Anglicans were specifically committed to facilitating the British colonization of the Paraguayan Chaco, most of which was probably owned by the British, as the land was sold on the London Stock Exchange. The Anglicans also had a mission in the Bolivian Chaco among the Izozog, which was closed down with the war. At the request of the Leach Brothers (also British), owners of the Esperanza sugar factory, the Anglicans spread their scope by creating Misión Chaqueña Algarrobal in 1914 near Embarcación, Salta,[8] and subsequently Misión San Andrés in 1927, along with numerous other missions in the western Chaco involving Mataco, Pilagá, and Toba Indians. The renowned Chaco linguist Richard Hunt, who initially worked in Paraguay among the Enxet, made his mark at Misión Chaqueña. The task of these missions was mainly focused on several forms of acculturation, especially the introduction of Christian teachings and values through the translation of the Bible into the vernacular languages.

Other Protestant missionary activity in the Paraguayan Chaco has been carried out throughout the twentieth century by the Mennonites, as well as by the New Tribes Mission.[9] Pentecostal missionary activity has also left its mark in the western Chaco, as evidenced by the Swedish Pentecostal work in Bolivia described by Alvarsson in chapter 2. Late in the twentieth century, other Catholic missions arrived in the area, such as the order of the Oblates of Mary Immaculate on the Pilcomayo and the Salesians on the Paraguay River.

Meanwhile, two Protestant mission compounds were established and disbanded for one reason or another among the Eastern Toba of northern Argentina: the British Emmanuel Mission in El Espinillo from 1934 to 1949 and the Mennonite Mission at Aguará from 1943 to 1955. A variety of other evangelical denominations, primarily Pentecostal in nature, established contacts with indigenous peoples of the southern Chaco region, but the vast majority of congregations currently active were started by indigenous leaders themselves with initial sponsorship by one denomination or another. The largest religious body in the region today, La Iglesia Evangélica Unida, has its own legal document with no ties to any external religious body, although Mennonite, Baptist, and Swedish Pentecostal missionaries currently serve as fraternal workers to the organization. The services consist of Pentecostal-type preaching, with stress on healing and Holy Spirit baptism that often entails a dance of "joy." The congregations are organized and administered by indigenous people themselves, primarily Eastern Toba, who initiated the organization with the assistance of post-Aguará Mennonite missionaries, but also by Mocoví, Pilagá, and Wichí. The indigenous church organization has reached into Paraguay and Bolivia as well in recent decades. Tensions between established church missions and this independent organization constitute a topic worthy of investigation.

CHACO INDIANS AND WAGE LABOR

Both when the military occupation was most aggressive against the Chaco Indians and when violence was concealed behind the idea of "pacification" leading to the supremacy of "law" and "progress," the processes that most deeply affected Gran Chaco peoples were related to their incorporation into the labor market. Such processes were characterized by seasonal or permanent migrations contributing in the final analysis to increasing sedentarization.

Sugar Factories

Already in the latter part of the nineteenth century, indigenous Chaco laborers were working on farms in eastern Tucumán, Jujuy, and Salta (Arenales 1833). With the introduction of industrial machinery, the economy of that area evolved toward extensive sugarcane cultivation, with a high demand for labor at harvest time. With the "pacification" of the region following the Victorica campaign of the mid-1880s, the Chaco Indians became the population called upon most directly to meet that need. Because the first factories needed a growing number of Indian workers, a novel hiring method was introduced based upon familiarity and acquaintance of some whites with the neighboring tribes. An expedition was organized with many gifts to be given away, and the appointed manager (*mayordomo*) marched deep into the Chaco to negotiate with Indian leaders about the hiring of "their" people. An Indian foreman placed in charge of commanding the factory workers was slowly displaced by an Indian interpreter who spoke the contact language and performed go-between functions.

In the early twentieth century, a sugar factory was also established in the eastern Chaco region of Argentina at Las Palmas, with the result that many local workers no longer traveled west to Tucumán and Salta. In both instances, however, an annual migratory rhythm to the plantations developed into a system of exchange not unlike the traditional one. The slow rhythm of the cane harvest was offset by the extremely high demographic concentration as well as by the abundance of goods provided. During the twentieth century, western sugar plantations modified their employment policy by hiring only criollo workers, mainly Bolivians, who were better disciplined and more dependent on their pay; they were more inclined to fully dedicate the whole day to work instead of dancing, getting drunk, or fighting. The Indians, in contrast, were happy to become wandering workers because this new modality allowed them to move and interact sporadically according to their own pleasure. The seasonal treks to sugar fields among some indigenous families came to be looked upon as a kind of festive occasion comparable to the *algarrobal* feasts of former times. In fact, a serious uprising at Colonia Napalpí in 1924 was sparked by the Chaco province governor's edict that Indians could no longer travel to Ledesma to harvest sugarcane because they were needed to pick the local cotton harvest. Nevertheless, the exploitation of Indian laborers in sugar and other Chaco industries has been well documented by writers such as Niklison (1916), Tolten (1936), García Pulido (1951), and Iñigo Carrera (1973), among others. In the Paraguayan Chaco, travel to the sugarcane fields by the Nivaclé was replaced by trips to the Mennonite colonies, where they began to settle and take on a variety of agricultural tasks.

Timber Industries

Together with the establishment of the first sugar factories in the western Chaco, a systematic and industrialized exploitation of the Chaco forest began in the east along the course of the Paraguay River. Many small and large entrepreneurs hired Indians to fell trees with axes. Among the preferred species were the *palo santo* (*Bulnesia*), the *algarrobo* (*Prosopis*), and the *quebracho* (*Schinopsis*). But the sawmills that altered Indian life most were those exploiting the *quebracho colorado* (*Schinopsis quebracho colorado*) to extract tannic acid for large international companies, such as La Forestal. Such undertakings required a large labor force, and many Indians, mostly Toba, were hired. These "woodcutters" incorporated into their culture not only the concepts related to the hiring and trading of their own workers, but also the dependence on "goods" usually given as part of their pay, which featured a series of manufactured products they came to incorporate permanently into their diet. This activity also brought about changes in the spatial distribution of Indian groups, for instance, when companies spread northward (Sastre-Casado), where *quebracho* extraction became highly significant in the Paraguayan Chaco as well. Casado, for example, is said to have owned nearly six thousand hectares and to have attracted large numbers of seasonal workers from far and near.

Agricultural Colonies

From the very start, agricultural activities, generally in conjunction with missionary endeavor, were seen as a means of converting the Indians into "civil life." Teaching European agricultural techniques was central to the colonial process of transculturation. In late nineteenth-century Argentina, the prevailing idea was that the rising waves of European settlers would mix with natives, both Indians and criollos, in the agricultural colonies. Here monoculture was practiced according to market demand at the time. Sugarcane, and later cotton in the eastern Chaco, were the raw materials for an incipient industrial development. Colonies of this nature were planned both for Europeans and for Indians. However, due to this policy, Indians soon became the population segment that provided labor for toiling the land and harvesting the crop, while the European landowners rapidly moved up the country's socioeconomic ladder.

Among the nineteenth century's settlement schemes figured the establishment of Colonia Rivadavia and the Córdoba native Domingo Astrada's subsequent founding of other colonies on the Pilcomayo. Thriving colonies like Castelli gave life to white villages and towns, whereas those located along the railway line, Bartolomé de las Casas, Juan Bautista Alberdi, and Francisco J. Muñiz, were less "successful" and therefore looked more like Indian villages.

During the first decades of the twentieth century, a number of flourishing rural colonies settled in the northern Chaco, marked primarily by the arrival of the Mennonites in 1927. Three colonies were established in Enxet and Enenxet territory, which soon attracted more Indians as the Mennonite economic development offered consistent jobs, albeit for low wages. Even today the Mennonites constitute a center of attraction for many indigenous groups, with a high percentage of Nivaclé and Enxet, although they summon other Indians as well, such as the Guaraní Ñandeva and Guaraní-Guarayo, Sanapaná, Angaité, and Ayoreo. Approximately 60 percent of the present-day Paraguayan Chaco Indian population is concentrated in the area of the Mennonite colonies.

Cattle Ranching

In Paraguay, the establishment of large cattle ranches permitted the creation of a symbiotic relationship between indigenous people and cattle owners. They worked on ranches but also continued to hunt and gather on the land. They also had access to ranch stores. This situation has changed drastically in the last twenty years with the creation of indigenous settlements. Families have left the ranches and moved onto the settlements, where they travel both to ranches and to the Mennonite colonies for work.

It should be noted that the extremely large ranches and extensive cattle ranching in Paraguay put much less pressure on the environment than elsewhere in the Chaco. This is now under threat as ranches are subdivided and exploitation becomes much more intense.[10]

In the southern Chaco of Argentina, a similar symbiotic process between indigenous people and cattlemen occurred, but in a much more limited sense and in a different form. In the Napalpí Reservation and Villa Ángela areas, for example, grasslands offered cattlemen an opportunity to take advantage of land allocated to Indians while acquiring cheap labor at the same time. However, the relationship was also symbiotic in that the cattlemen offered Toba and Mocoví families resources they otherwise would not have acquired.

SEDENTARIZATION PROCESSES

As the rivers became increasingly navigable during the late eighteenth and nineteenth centuries, and railroads were established throughout the Gran Chaco region in the twentieth century, often with Indian labor, the economy of Bolivia was linked with the lower Pilcomayo and Bermejo rivers, and it became possible to transport Indian and criollo laborers more efficiently to sugar and cotton fields. Meanwhile, European settlement in agricultural colonies forced the Indian communities into smaller and smaller pockets of land, making it impossible to survive on traditional hunting and collecting technologies alone. This increasing external pressure throughout the twentieth century obliged indigenous families to become more and more sedentarized as they lost access to territory where they were accustomed to seasonally roam. Such mobility was related to their economy and functionally necessary for the reproduction of the Gran Chaco social model.

Throughout this process, Indians gradually lost contact with their territory, discontinuing or disrupting the set of integrated habits and activities that had thus far characterized their cultures. The two determining factors contributing to this process, then, were (1) white occupation of the land, initially effected by the establishment of missions and later by governmental policy attracting immigrants to colonize the region for agricultural purposes, and (2) the resulting dependence upon Indian wage labor. As demands for wage labor decreased in the latter twentieth century, due to crop failures and increasing mechanization, increasingly large numbers of Argentine Chaco Indians have moved to urban centers, not only in the southern Chaco itself, but as far away as Santa Fe, Rosario, Buenos Aires, and even La Plata. In Paraguay, on the other hand, movement to towns has been minimal, perhaps due to the attraction of jobs and settlement in the Mennonite colonies area. The one clear exception to this observation concerns the Maká, who were taken to Asunción a long time ago, where they settled and live off the tourist trade.

Because each of the many social groups and territories occupied in the past operated somewhat as an organic whole, the sedentarization process in which most of the groups lost access to land previously available to them is synonymous with the disorganization of Indian societies. The appearance is that of an infectious bleeding, which thickens and lumps at different points with no chance of coagulation. This process threatens the survival of Gran Chaco peoples unless alternative solutions are found.

THE PRESENT SITUATION

Today Gran Chaco Indians make up heterogeneous groups of people whose apparent unity springs from the asymmetric relationship they maintain with the global society. Their present situation throughout the Southern Cone is highly dynamic. Apart from the mass migration to cities and the gradual urbanization process with its overwhelming impact upon the cultures, the last few years have seen a radical change in the legal tradition of South American countries that is apparently geared toward ethnic tolerance and the acceptance of somewhat autonomous governments for each of these peoples. On the other hand, the transformation of the Gran Chaco habitat, mainly as a result of criollo cattle grazing, one of the primary causes of ecological deterioration in the region, but also due to deforestation and an overproduction of cotton, has radically curtailed the possibility of maintaining the traditional sustenance model.[11]

Of all the Chaco populations, only small groups of Ayoreo found in northern Paraguay have managed to avoid submission to the global society. The last uncontacted group of Ayoreo, found just to the north of the Mennonite colonies, is known as Totobiegosode; it is estimated that about thirty of them remain in the forest. The others were captured in 1979 and 1986 by the New Tribes Mission and evangelized enemy Ayoreo. In Paraguay, the majority of Ayoreo work in the Mennonite colonies. Among the rest, a minority lives in rural communities set up at the time of sedentarization, but even these people maintain ties to kin living primarily in the suburbs of small and middle-sized white towns, as well as to an ever-increasing number living in the outskirts of major cities. It would appear that the latter number will rapidly increase unless changes introduced by recent legislation will succeed in offsetting their unfavorable situation.

Although political participation of indigenous peoples in the three countries is provided for, it has thus far been passive. One reason is that their political customs are so utterly different from the participative democracy of the Southern Cone governments that Indians have merely negotiated their vote, with the unfortunate consequences involved. Now that legal reform is under way, there is hope that in the future Indian peoples might be better represented and their interests no longer ignored.

In the 1980s the countries making up the Gran Chaco embarked on a process of legal reform. The starting point for a series of initiatives was an agreement on aboriginal and tribal peoples signed within the framework of the International Labor Organization (OIT). This new legislation, known as Convention 169, has been ratified by Bolivia and Paraguay and incorporated into national law by Argentina, but its ratification has not been deposited in Geneva. Nevertheless, it does show a clear trend toward giving indigenous minorities gradual autonomy. It also introduces changes in the rules governing landownership in force until the 1980s and confers on the Indians varying degrees of participation in the management of natural resources. These changes consider the collective ownership of some kinds of property, which up to now has not been clearly defined, and the right to bilingual education and a set of rights for cultural conservation. Such legal changes imply a deep transformation in the relations between Indians and the nation-states upon which they depend, and manifest a growing awareness among majorities of the need for restoring, at least in part, the justice that has been denied to indigenous peoples.[12]

NOTES

1. That is, they have become confined to delimited territories, although family members make claims to available alternative space in country and city so that considerable movement from place to place continues to the present time.

2. The Mbayá, now known as the Caduveo, no longer live in the Chaco region, but in Mato Grosso.

3. Cabrera and Willink 1973:72–73; Ragonese and Castiglioni 1970:142–154; Arenas 1981.

4. The arrival of the horse in the Chaco is a topic that generates considerable debate. The question is whether it arrived via Santa Fe, as Metraux (1946:202–203) and others have suggested, or whether it appeared considerably earlier via Tucumán, which would explain early indigenous equestrian skills. Schindler (1985) has argued convincingly against the idea that the horse was used for hunting purposes.

5. As noted previously, these people are now located in Mato Grosso where they are known as Caduveo.

6. Stephen Kidd, author of chapter 3, prefers to speak of exogamous ego-centered kindreds rather than of bands and tribes (personal correspondence).

7. However, note Miller's argument (chapter 6) for a newly developing ethnic consciousness among the Toba that incorporates a more regional grouping based upon common language and values.

8. This mission was also founded by Grubb.

9. For a discussion of Mennonite and indigenous relations, see Redekop 1980.

10. Personal correspondence from Stephen Kidd.

11. Livestock increased from 273,129 animals in 1888 to 4,519,324 a century later; herds became sixteen times larger, and the number of cattle per square kilometer went from 0.7 to 12 (see Neddermann 1987:9–10, who points out that in the Chaco province of Argentina alone, herds grew from 83,952 heads in 1895 to 1,094,260 in 1960; see also Morello and Adámoli 1968).

12. While the indigenous legislation in the three countries has been good, what remains to be seen is how much interest there is in its actual implementation. In Paraguay, indigenous people still have less than 2 percent of the Chaco land and mainly live in overpopulated colonies.

REFERENCES

Arenales, José. 1833. *Noticias históricas y descriptivas sobre el gran país del Chaco y Río Bermejo: Con observaciones relativas a un plan de navegación y colonización que se propone*. Buenos Aires: Imprenta Hallet y Cía.

Arenas, Pastor. 1981. *Etnobotánica Lengua-Maskoy*. Buenos Aires: FECYC (Fundació para la Educación, la Ciencia, y la Cultura).

Bartolomé, Leopoldo. 1972. Movimientos milenaristas de los aborígenes chaqueños entre 1903 y 1933. *Suplemento Antropológico* 7(1–2): 107–120.

Braunstein, José. 1983. *Algunos rasgos de la organización social de los indígenas del Gran Chaco*. Trabajos de Etnología, Publicación no. 2. Buenos Aires: Instituto de Ciencias Antropológicas, Universidad de Buenos Aires.

Cabrera, Angel L., and Abraham Willink. 1973. *Biogeografía de América Latina*. Serie de Biología, Monografía no. 13. Washington, D.C.: OAS.

García Pulido, José. 1951. *El Gran Chaco y su imperio Las Palmas*. Resistencia: Casa García.

Iñigo Carrera, Nicolás. 1973. Génesis de un semiproletariado rural: La incorporación de los indígenas a la producción algodonera chaqueña. Buenos Aires: Centro de Investigaciones en Ciencias Sociales, Quadernos, Serie Estudios 4.

Métraux, Alfred. 1946. Ethnography of the Chaco. In *Handbook of South American Indians*, ed. J. Steward, 1:197–370. Washington, D.C.: Smithsonian Institution, Bureau of American Ethology.

Miller, Elmer S. 1977. Shamanism and Leadership in the Gran Chaco: A Dynamic View. American Anthropological Association Meetings, Houston, Texas, November. Published in *Working Papers on South American Indians*, No. 4:5–10. Bennington, Vt.: Bennington College, 1992.

Morello, Jorge, and Jorge Adámoli. 1968. *La vegetación de la República Argentina. Las grandes unidades de vegetación y ambiente del Chaco Argentino. Primera parte: Objetivos y metodología*. Serie Fitogeografía No. 10. Buenos Aires: I.N.T.A.

Neddermann, Ursula Irene. 1987. Evolución de la actividad ganadera en el Chaco entre 1900 y 1952. *Cuadernos de Geohistoria Regional* 20:9–10. Resistencia: Instituto de Investigaciones Geohistóricas de Conícet.

Niklison, José E. 1916. Investigación en los Territorios Federales del Chaco y Formosa. In *Boletín del Departamento Nacional del Trabajo* 34(2), libros 3–4. Buenos Aires: Imprenta de la Policía.

Ragonese, Arturo, and Julio Castiglioni. 1970. Vegetación del parque chaqueño. *Boletín de la Sociedad Argentina de Botánica* 11, Suplemento.

Redekop, Calvin. 1980. *Strangers Become Neighbors: Mennonite and Indigenous Relations in the Paraguayan Chaco*. Scottdale, Pa.: Herald Press.

Schindler, Helmut. 1985. Equestrian and Non-Equestrian Indians of the Gran Chaco during the Colonial Period. *Indiana* 10:451–464.

Schmidel, Ulderico. 1534–54. Viaje al Río de la Plata. In *Colección de obras y documentos relativos a la historia antigua y moderna de las provincias del Río de la Plata*, ed. Pedro de Angelis, 6:261–346. Buenos Aires: Editorial Plus Ultra, 1970.

Tolten, Hans. 1936. *Enchanting Wilderness. Adventures in Darkest South America*. Translated from German by Fredi Loesch. London: Selwyn and Blount.

2

Foraging in Town: Survival Strategies among the 'Weenhayek of Bolivia and Argentina

Jan-Åke Alvarsson

THE ARMADILLO

The sun is slowly setting. Nolnejen and I are in the driver's cab.[1] We are on our way home to Tuntey after a trip to the 'Weenhayek villages along the Pilcomayo.[2] (Map 3 shows the location of the majority of the 'Weenhayek villages.) The jeep's platform is full of people who are eager to get a free ride up to town. The track varies notably as it takes us through high forest, salt plains, and palm groves. Here and there the road disappears. The river has cut a new course and has taken part of the old track with it. We have to cut a new way through the bush; our eyes are intensely fixed on the roadway to discover sharp-edged stumps or deep holes.

Suddenly an armadillo toddles out of the brush, heading for an open glade on the other side of the tracks. You don't see an armadillo that often, and I have always taken a keen interest in animals, so I slam on the brakes. "Let's catch it!" I yell to Nolnejen. All of a sudden we are out of the car, the motor still running, trying to catch up with the armadillo.

Without a word we fall into a traditional form of pair hunting. We let the armadillo run in a zigzag pattern between us to tire it out and, most important, not give it time to dig itself into the ground.

The hunt is over in a few minutes. The armadillo obviously gets increasingly tired, and at a turn Nolnejen jumps at it. He gets it with his right hand and slows it down.

"Hold it there!" I say and run to the car to get my camera. In a minute I have the hunter posing with the *jwoqatsaj*, a nine-banded armadillo (*Dasypus noremcintus*). It turns out to be a nice picture: Nolnejen, my good friend and informant, in the middle of the dry forest of the Gran Chaco, gently holding

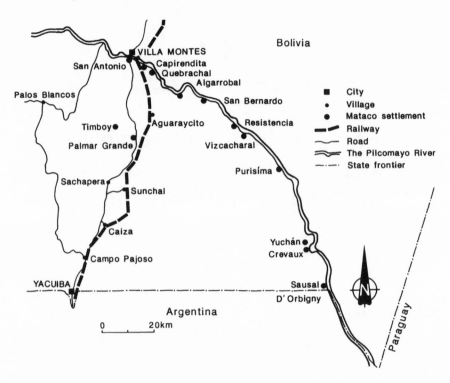

Map 3. 'Weenhayek Settlements in the Bolivian Chaco Central

one of the most common bags of the 'Weenhayek Indians. I am very pleased, and without even reflecting on the consequences, I ask him to let it go.

For me, this is the only natural outcome. I have been brought up in northern Europe and have been taught to treat animals with respect ever since I was a small boy.[3] My years among the Field Biologists of Sweden further reinforced that attitude.[4] I am a true lover of animals. I would not even kill a poisonous snake if it were not threatening.

"Okay, let it go!" I repeat.

Nolnejen slowly loosens the grip of his hand and glances furtively at me. His eyes are full of confusion, but he obviously sees me as the boss. I am the one paying him for teaching me the 'Weenhayek language. He reluctantly lets go. The armadillo looks surprised. It takes a while before it realizes it is again free to disappear into the brush.

Not until I turn around do I understand what I have done. The full load of people from the jeep's platform is standing in a semicircle behind me. Their eyes do not express admiration for what we have done. On the contrary, they display stupefaction, disappointment, and possibly irritation.

It takes me some time before I realize the implications of what has happened. At first I only register the obvious cultural confrontation. These people have just seen their supper trot away. Armadillos could be compared to our own fast food. When one is caught, it is killed by a stroke in the neck. Then it is placed upside down on the fire and cooked in its own shell. The only thing you have to do is to wait, and that time you spend chatting with friends, not staring at the wall like most people do in fast-food lines at home.

As I think about it while I drive home, it becomes increasingly clear to me that Nolnejen and I reacted almost instinctively. There is a hunting drive in all of us. Sometimes it pops up when we see a football and a goal; at other times when we are in some kind of contest.[5] Even university professors display this when they compete for a position.

But in Western society, this drive has been diffused and is hard to discern. We may even hide it under covers called "charity" or "patriotic deeds." Among the 'Weenhayek, however, this drive is employed for what it probably was intended in the beginning: maintaining one's family. This was the main reason for the culture shock. While I was pleased to preserve nature, Nolnejen just saw me throwing a new-bought hamburger into the dustbin.

The readiness Nolnejen displayed when he saw the armadillo is an example of something just as basic in human nature: opportunism. Hunters and gatherers have survived for millennia in almost all ecological niches of the world just because they lean on opportunism, not specialization. While a Western hunter goes deer hunting or moose hunting, a 'Weenhayek Indian just goes *kyowalhan* (roaming the forest) or, using the technical equivalent, "foraging." This means that he, because it is always a man that goes hunting, takes his machete, slings his string bag over his shoulder, and departs for the forest with his dog.

In the forest, he is alert to whatever may appear. He might see a tiny bee that could lead him to honey. He will probably find tracks, some of them fresh enough to follow. But his hope is for something else: that during the day, something unusual, something unexpected, will turn up. It is at that single moment that he has to know enough and to have enough self-control to take advantage of the situation. "That was my luck," he may say afterwards if he has succeeded.

Opportunism does not work without a skilled and alert actor. To be able to survive on hunting and gathering in a dry and barren wilderness like the northern Gran Chaco, a person needs deep knowledge about the flora and the fauna of the region. But mere classification is in itself useless. One needs to know how the different species behave (ethology) and how to interact with them (ecology). I have often marveled at the deep knowledge of virtually everything in the forest that 'Weenhayek men display. Furthermore, one needs to develop physical skills: swiftness, strength, and endurance. Mental

skills, like patience, intuition, and improvisation, are important comple-
ments. In our stereotypes of foragers, we picture them as somewhat lazy because they do not work as many hours as we do. In this perspective, it is
interesting to note that among themselves, the 'Weenhayek always rank in-
dustriousness as the most important trait when judging a fellow human
being, and not without reason; they know what it takes to survive.

Male hunting opportunism is not the only endemic strategy, however.
Women demonstrate a different type of opportunism. While men seem to be
relegated to the more uncertain margins of nature and culture, obviously because those niches also have to be exploited, women concentrate on more secure resources. When they leave for the forest in the morning, they seem to
know exactly where they are heading. A grove of trees is full of fruits. They
walk there, fill their *sikyetis* (carrying nets), and depart for home. In the af-
ternoon, a woman leaves for a tree that fell last year. Now it is dry enough
for firewood. She piles up as much as she can carry, winds a fiber cord
around it, and brings it to the village on her back.

While men are socialized to seize the opportunity, women are trained to
locate resources. While it is possible to generalize on the basis of men's
knowledge, women's knowledge is far more specific. Their opportunism is
based on their knowledge about when and where to find ripe fruits, berries,
nuts, rhizomes, roots, and the like. Thus they are able to provide the bulk of
what the family needs to eat. While men come home with an occasional bag
that means feast, women carry home something to eat every day.

This division of labor is one of the basic foundations of 'Weenhayek society, as it is of most other foraging societies. If resources are scarce, one cannot waste time discussing who is going to do what. Women bear and
breast-feed children. Therefore, they cannot be away from home for more
than a couple of hours at a time. Men have parental duties as well, but they
are more free to be absent for longer periods and to take on more dangerous
activities. To survive its first years, a small child needs its mother more than
it does its father.

Lately, we in the West have come to view division of labor according to
sex as something oppressive. Men and women should do the same things
and consequently divide the rewards equally. Among the 'Weenhayek, the
opposite is the natural thing. Almost everything is divided between the sexes,
and the division is reinforced by taboos. If a man would do a woman's
work, he might face supernatural retribution.

THE *ALGARROBO* TREE

During the majority of the six years that I have spent among the 'Weenhayek, I have lived in a house located between the Indian camp and the mestizo section of Tuntey.[6] That constitutes, indeed, a symbolic position. The
mestizos find me odd because I dedicate most of my time to the totally irrel-

evant and uninteresting Indians when there are so many other interesting things to be explored in life. In the eyes of the 'Weenhayek, I am almost as odd. It is true that I take a keen interest in their lives, have a great many friends, and speak their language. In this respect, I am different from most other whites. But I am not an Indian, and I never will become one.

I am considered to be a type of quasi-'Weenhayek. I have several 'Weenhayek names. I am regarded as the foremost expert on string-bag designs. Women may even ask me about the name of some of them. I might even qualify as their historian par excellence. They know that I know more about 'Weenhayek culture than most 'Weenhayek. But I look too different. My language will never become perfect, and I cannot deny that I am also a part of another world.

Outside this border house, there is a huge *algarrobo* tree (*Prosopis alba*), in 'Weenhayek called *jwaayukw*, freely translated as "the container of *jwaay*," or *algarroba* pods. Like many other phenomena in this culture, it is classified according to its nutritive contribution. A tree is thus a "container of fruit," while a bee is a mere "keeper of honey."

In November or December, these yellow fruits ripen and offer a juicy, sweet taste that reminds me of the cream toffees of my childhood. They are not only tasty, but rich in protein, and they brew a strong beer if fermented. As if this were not enough, they may ripen in quantities large enough to feed a multitude.[7] This has made *jwaay* the most popular vegetable of the Chaco.

When these fruits ripen, 'Weenhayek women approach the trees with long sticks, beat down the tree fruits, and gather them in their *sikyetis*. For the pods at the top, one is dependent upon the strong squalls that often appear at dawn during the fruit season. In the morning, a woman may load her *sikyet* full of *jwaay* in a few minutes.

A sign of this fruit's popularity is shown by the fact that I rarely, if ever, have been able to eat any fruit from the tree outside my house. However early I wake up, someone seems to have been there before me. Every *yakyup* (fruit season, which is summer) I have had the same expectations: "This year I will eat my fill of those full and abundant pods." Every time the same scenario repeats itself. The closest I have come to the yellow pods is a glance at the cloths full of pods that the children are carrying away when I go out.

The abundance of tree fruits during *yakyup* has been one of the most important parts of the social life of the Chaco Indians. Their opportunism has demanded that they live in small bands for most of the year, enabling them to divide the territory and successfully exploit the meager resources. But during the fruit season, it has been possible to gather the whole *wikyi'* (extended-family group) at a single location. This was the social "high season" of the 'Weenhayek and other Amerindian peoples of the Chaco.[8] During this period, they could brew large quantities of *algarroba* beer. This filling beer could satisfy a hundred people or more, enabling them to chat, fight, sing, dance, and perform rituals.

As the food was available at a single location, time could be dedicated entirely to social and ritual activities. It was a time when people could bury those who had died during the dry season when the earth was too hard to dig up,[9] perform initiation rituals for girls who had had their first menstruation, or celebrate newly formed matrimonial pairings. It was also a time when young people from the different bands, or even from other *wikyi*'s, could meet and form new relations that eventually could lead to marriage.

But the fruit season was limited. Once it was over, people had to split up and move out to other locations where the "emergency foods" were to be found in limited quantities. During the period that followed, very little was to be found in the forest. Thus the skills of the hunter were to be tested. A "trial marriage" was literally put to the test not too many weeks after the sequence of beer parties.

Mobility is a key word in foraging societies, and this condition is reflected in many aspects of 'Weenhayek culture. The most striking to the eye is the fact that there are no permanent buildings, no large constructions, and no heavy items at all. Nowadays, people use wooden mortars, but in the old days a hole in the ground, covered with a skin, would have to do. A wooden mortar was far too heavy to carry along.

Thus artistic skills were never demonstrated in architecture. Instead, people specialized in small-scale art. Men painted their faces for the dances. They carved in wood. They burned designs into bows, arrows, calabashes, and the like. Women tattooed themselves. They also sewed beautiful clothes and wove *caraguatá* string bags and filled them with beautiful and intricate geometrical designs. They gave them appealing names after mythological animals or plants. One was called Ahutsaj after a daring bird and a courageous culture hero. Another was called "snake's back" after its zigzag pattern.

THE WOMAN IS THE ACTIVE PARTY

Mobility also meant that one of the partners in a marriage had to separate from one's original family. Among the 'Weenhayek, it was the man. It was easier for him to move. His knowledge of nature was more general. He was used to long trips and had probably gone hunting before in the territory of his new family, or at least in similar landscapes. Uxorilocality was, therefore, and is still the rule for postmarital residence.

Among the 'Weenhayek, since time immemorial it has been considered natural that the woman, not the man, as among ourselves, should take the initiative in an affair and eventually in marriage. During the dances at the *jwaay* parties, it was therefore the man who adorned himself, painted his face, combed his long, shining hair, and put on all his necklaces, breast bands, most beautiful clothes, and ankle bands. In the evening, he started to dance with his friends, and they kept dancing until the young women eventually showed up and chose partners.

Once selected, the young man could do little but comply with the desires of the woman. If he did not like her, the only outlet he had was to escape from her before she woke up in the morning. If he did like her, however, he followed her to her home and lived with his parents-in-law for some time. The latter put him to the test even while he took a close look at the skills of the woman. If both parties were satisfied with what they saw, a more stable liaison, "marriage," could take place.

FISH FEVER

When natural resources are limited, an occasional spell of affluence is regarded as something irresistible. One such instance of plenty is the fish season among the 'Weenhayek.[10] In the days before the Chaco War in the 1930s, it meant good eating of fat and abundant food. From the beginning of the 1970s, it has also meant quick money and temporary economic affluence. From then on, the 'Weenhayek have sold fish to truck drivers and entrepreneurs who transport them up to the highlands and in turn sell them on the national market.

This period can be detected as "fish fever" in many 'Weenhayek men. I became acutely aware of that myself the first year I worked with Nolnejen. After the fruit season, we had met almost every day and studied the language together. Because he could not take on any other work while he taught me, I found it natural that he should be paid, so I did.

But if you pay someone to do a job for you, you enter into a type of employer-employee relationship and develop mutual expectations. So I expected Nolnejen to be working with me on a daily basis, now that I paid him. When we were actually starting to "take off," he suddenly did not appear anymore. He had asked for permission to visit a fishing camp for two days, which I naturally granted him. But he never came back. Once in the camp, he was hit by fish fever and could not resist. He did not return until the fishing season was over.

Later I discovered that if a 'Weenhayek man ignores the fishing season, it is considered something incredibly surprising. Another of my friends, Noqnumhnahen, did that once in the 1980s when he fabricated wickerlike furniture instead and made enough money on that. He also disliked slipping into the cold water now that he was in his fifties, although he had been fishing his whole life. Nevertheless, this was still considered something inconceivable.

KEEPING THE KEEPERS HAPPY

Opportunism does not mean only taking all the openings that nature offers. Somehow it means being active and maintaining interaction with the Keepers of Nature, *Lawolh*.[11] These are true supernatural beings. Much more potent than human beings, they belong to another dimension. Nevertheless, they are there to be exploited by man if he is capable of doing so.

In the 'Weenhayek cosmos, there are vestiges of a distant creator, *Lham-t-'ihi'-pule'* (He-who-is-in-the sky). He is there and might help a fisherman if he is being pulled down by some underwater monster in the river. Otherwise, he plays an insignificant role in 'Weenhayek everyday life.

Instead, a group of intermediate spiritual functionaries play the main parts. These are sometimes called "Lords of Nature" by historians of religion. That term gives me wrong associations, however, so on the basis of the 'Weenhayek term, *-wo'* (one who takes care of; one in charge of), I prefer the term "keepers."

To the Indians, these "Keepers" are not a mere category, but individuals. They are called by descriptive names, just like humans: Eteksayntaj (head-of-lichens), Ky'utsetaj (*caraguatá*-big), and so on. According to the 'Weenhayek worldview, each one is in charge of a certain sector of nature, such as a category of particular plants needed for handicraft or important game animals.

This means that in everyday life it is just as natural to watch out for a "Keeper" as for rain or thunder. It also signifies that one should respect a long series of taboos, like reconstructing a bee's nest after having taken the honey or not littering with leaves from the *caraguatá* plant after having taken what one needs. If a person were to disregard these rules, he would at first be stricken with, perhaps, momentary blindness. If he persisted, he might face permanent blindness or even death.

When a man goes big-game hunting, he had better contact the "Keeper" in advance to get permission. Sometimes he needs the *hiyawu'* (shaman) to do that for him. But if he goes for peccaries, he should also know which ones he can fell, because all the big "silverbacks" belong to Eteksayntaj. Should he not respect this rule, he is in for harsh supernatural treatment.

In 'Weenhayek life, there is a very thin line, if any, between the "natural" and the "supernatural." It is, in fact, more productive to speak about "nature" and "culture" instead, where the first includes our category for supernatural and the second comprises everything that belongs to the unnamed domestic sector. We might put the label *wikyiwet* (the place of humans) on it, but lexically that is only used for a "village." 'Weenhayek culture, like the earth layer where humans and "Keepers" live, lacks a name.[12] It is simply taken for granted.

The form of respect that the 'Weenhayek show toward the "Keepers" is an interesting matter. It is in fact akin to that which they show for old people. Often I feel that it is a matter of manipulating the "Keepers" so that humans can get as much out of them as possible. Negotiating with a "Keeper" has very little resemblance to the humble attitude toward the divine that we find in most world religions. Instead, human beings may cheat, lie, flatter, or do whatever they find necessary to achieve what is needed, that is, resources to survive.

FORAGING IN TOWN

Before the Chaco War in the 1930s, the Bolivian 'Weenhayek had very little contact with whites.[13] During the war, however, this changed drastically. For a couple of years, white officers and Andean soldiers were swarming like bees in the Chaco. The 'Weenhayek, who were unable to grasp the logic of the fight, called it the "War of the Whites." Their reluctance to enter the war on the Bolivian side gained them a reputation for being suspect, and therefore they were put in concentration camps.

In these camps, they became accustomed to white foods like sugar, mate, rice, and macaroni. When the war was over, little remained in the forests, so many 'Weenhayek moved to town. Most of them settled in Tuntey, the place the whites call Villa Montes. There they could continue the patron-client relationships that they had established during the war and find the goods that they had become accustomed to. They put up a temporary camp by the river, just as if they had been fishing or foraging in that region.

When they went into town, they used the same strategies as when they were foraging. They were open for whatever might happen, and when something did occur, they seized the opportunity, whether it was a *changa* (a temporary job) or something given as charity to the "poor Indian." If this was money, it was quickly transformed into food, preferably sugar, mate, macaroni, or rice. Parts of the wages were paid in kind, however, usually in tobacco, alcohol, or coca leaves. The 'Weenhayek were already passionate smokers, but an increasing number became addicted to alcohol and coca.

In the 1940s something happened that successively altered the situation. First, only a single white woman, unlike the rest, appeared and sided with the Indians. She was a missionary, but not a Catholic. The 'Weenhayek had had bad experiences with Catholic fathers of previous missionary attempts, and they were hesitant to repeat those experiences. Therefore, the fact that she was not a Bolivian nor a Catholic was important to them. "La Hermana Astrid," as she was called, came to gain the confidence of the Indians.[14]

A FAMILY OF "KEEPERS"

In a few years a family appeared: husband, wife, and children. They were called the Flood family.[15] The man was an entrepreneur, and the Indians quickly learned to make use of his persuasive skills. He was the first person to obtain land for the 'Weenhayek. They came to respect him, much as they respected the "Keepers." They turned to him to organize transportation, they asked him to persuade the authorities, and they complained to him if they were maltreated.

The missionaries were against addiction. Harsh clashes of interests occurred when the other whites wanted to pay the Indians in kind, as they had always done, and the male missionary demanded that they stop. If the Indians were to live in the Christian Indian camp on "liberated land," they had to give up the drugs. If they gave up drugs, he would help them to sell their handicrafts; he would help them to sell their fish; he would get more land. In a fairly short time, Lhapuhwjwa' Flood had surpassed Eteksayntaj in importance. Not that the one was able to eradicate reliance on the other (as he probably hoped), but, in the altered situation after the Chaco War, more aid and support seemed to reach the Indians through the first than through the second "Keeper."

The end result is, in fact, even more surprising. The foragers who were effectively tied to whites during the Chaco War were successively and successfully detached from white society with the help of the missionaries. Through teetotal abstinence from drugs, they could break with apathy and subordination to those distributing drugs. Through contributions like the commercialization of fishing and handicrafts, men as well as women regained an economic independence that made it possible to cut dependence on former patron-client relationships. Through education, they have lately even liberated themselves from the dependence on missionaries.

When I came to the Chaco for the first time in the 1970s, traditional foraging strategies were still readily observable. Something that became more and more obvious to me was that both male and female strategies were maintained also in this foreign environment. Men went for the uncertain changas; they could wait for hours, sometimes even days, at a street corner to get a temporary job, in or outside of town. When and whenever they got something, they quickly transformed it into food and brought it home.[16]

Women, however, would use the direct gathering method. They would walk up to a person, or to the home of someone they knew, and insist. They would offer to wash laundry, to get water, or to do something else that they knew that person needed. If she or he did not need anything, they would insist on alms. They quickly learned how much they could expect and organized their gathering of payment or alms just as they would a day in the bush.[17] More or less on time, they would be back with their families to feed them.

In the 1980s this has slowly changed. Today, the ethnolinguistic group of the 'Weenhayek stands stronger than ever before during the century. New villages, organized according to a traditional pattern, have been founded. Leaders of the old type, niyat, have resurged. No 'Weenhayek has any permanent employment outside the mission or with other nongovernmental organizations (NGOs) or Indian organizations.[18] The people have gained the legal right to traditional 'Weenhayek land.[19] Officially, the ethnolinguistic group has become accepted as a nation in its own right. Even the Pentecostal church that was introduced by the missionaries, now called the Iglesia 'Weenhayek, has increasingly Indianist tendencies. It is becoming more and more important in carving out a reborn 'Weenhayek identity.[20] In sum, the 'Weenhayek are again free to roam the *kyowalhan* (forest), as they have done for millennia, following the ancient survival strategies that we associate with the traditional "foraging mind."

NOTES

1. Ignacio Nolnejen Pérez was my first head informant (1976–77). My second main informant was Celestino Manhyejas Gómez (1978–79, 1982–83). This chapter is based on more than six years of fieldwork with the 'Weenhayek Indians over a period of more than two decades. Ever since January 1976 I have been in constant contact with my 'Weenhayek friends.

The 'Weenhayek Indians are the northernmost of the Mataco peoples, the vast majority living in Bolivia. They were formerly called the Mataco-Noctenes. Rafael Karsten (1932:26) defined them thusly: "The third tribe, called Mataco-Noctenes [*sic*], occupies the great triangle roughly formed by lines connecting the villages Yacuiba, Villa Montes and Crevaux." The name derives from the denomination *weenha-lhame* (different), a term that was initially used as a derogatory name for the northernmost dialect group of the Mataco peoples ("The Different Ones"). With time, the 'Weenhayek themselves have adopted this denomination and now see it as something (positively) characteristic: "We are not like them, we are different" is a common statement. The name Mataco has become increasingly controversial, however. The 'Weenhayek erroneously, at least from an etymological perspective, conclude that it is an ascribed name related to the Spanish verb *matar* (to kill), which they find repulsive. This is also the reason I successively have come to adopt the denomination 'Weenhayek in my writings.

2. Tuntey is the 'Weenhayek name for Villa Montes. I use it here to denote that we are moving in an Amerindian cosmos that was established long before the whites came here, and even longer before the Bolivian president Ismael Montes came to visit and give this place its name around 1910.

3. I was born and raised in Sweden, where animal activism is unusually common and the majority of the population are lovers of animals.

4. The Field Biologists (Swedish Fältbiologerna) is a youth organization associated with the Swedish Association for the Conservation of Nature. Its activities include field excursions, bird watching, and the like.

5. The English sociobiologist Desmond Morris, for example, has likened today's soccer games to classic collective hunting (Morris 1982:451), or to traditional fights between rivaling groups (1982:195).

6. I had a house in Tuntey (Villa Montes) that served as the base for my family. I also had a house in Ho'o'yo', however, a distant, isolated village that I used to obtain comparative information. In my Ho'o'yo' house I lived for anything from a couple of days up to two weeks at a time.

7. Erland Nordenskiöld provided a vivid description of these *algarroba* parties in his book *Indianliv* (1926:77ff.). See also Métraux 1946:350.

8. This could be compared with the social "high season" of the Ese Ejja bands of the Amazon region, who gather at a single location when the river turtles lay their eggs, or the Fuegian peoples, who gathered when a whale was stranded at one of the beaches. In all three cases, the economic base for large gatherings was utilized to perform social and ritual activities.

9. This form of secondary burials has been described by Métraux (1946:329, illustration on p. 352a1—Plate 70).

10. The fishing season extends from May to September, with a peak from June to August (see Alvarsson 1988:59, 182–189, 292–296).

11. *Lawolh* is the plural form; in the singular the word is *lawo'*, with a glottal stop at the end. The central morpheme is *-wo'* (one who takes care of; one in charge of), which implies a translation akin to "keeper of" in a very general sense.

12. The 'Weenhayek cosmos is divided into three main layers, the underworld, the overworld, and the central earth layer. These were once connected, but in mythic times the "sin" of man destroyed these connections (see Alvarsson 1988:49ff.).

13. The Chaco War took place from 1932 to 1935 (see Alvarsson 1988:29–30).

14. *La hermana* translates "sister." The woman's full name was Astrid Jansson. She was a representative of the Swedish Free Mission (Misión Sueca Libre en Bolivia) and started work in Villa Montes in 1943. For a general assessment of evangelical missionary work among the Mataco peoples, see Fock (1966/67:97).

15. Gustav and Marta Flood, also members of the Swedish Free Mission.

16. Palavecino stated that a Mataco Indian "hunts his day labor wage" (1958–59:384), thus indicating that he uses the same basic strategy and has the same type of expectations, "immediate return," as when hunting in the forest. For a discussion of "immediate return," see Woodburn 1991.

17. The Argentinean scholar José Braunstein has observed the same behavior in Las Lomitas (personal communication).

18. For a full account of change and continuity in 'Weenhayek society, see Alvarsson 1998.

19. In 1992 a group of geographers, lawyers, and anthropologists (including myself) delimited and established the blueprint for a 'Weenhayek independent territory. The law confirming the establishment was passed by the Bolivian government in 1993.

20. For an account of the new 'Weenhayek church, see Alvarsson 1998.

REFERENCES

Alvarsson, Jan-Åke. 1988. *The Mataco of the Gran Chaco: An Ethnographic Account of Change and Continuity in Mataco Socio-Economic Organization.* Uppsala Studies in Cultural Anthropology 11. Uppsala and Stockholm: Almqvist & Wiksell International.

———. 1998. True Pentecostals or True Amerindians—or Both? Religious Identity among the 'Weenhayek Indians of Southern Bolivia. In *Religions in Transition: Mobility, Merging and Globalization in the Emergence of Contemporary Religious Identities*, ed. Jan-Åke Alvarsson and Rita Laura Segato, pp. 174–192. Uppsala: Uppsala University.

Fock, Niels. 1966/67. Mataco Indians in Their Argentine Setting. *Folk* 8–9:89–104.

Karsten, Rafael. 1932. *Indian Tribes of the Argentine and Bolivian Chaco: Ethnological Studies*. Societas Scientiarum Fennica, Commentationes Humanarum Litterarum 4, 1. Helsinki: Akademische Buchhandlung.

Métraux, Alfred. 1946. Ethnography of the Chaco. In *Handbook of South American Indians*, ed. Julian H. Steward, 1:197–370. Washington, D.C.: Smithsonian Institution, Bureau of American Ethnology.

Morris, Desmond. 1982. *The Pocket Guide to Manwatching*. London: Granada Press.

Nordenskiöld, Erland. 1926. *Indianliv i El Gran Chaco (Syd-Amerika)*. Stockholm: Ahlén & Akerlundi.

Palavecino, Enrique. 1958–59. Algunas notas sobre la transculturación del indío chaqueño. *Runa* (Buenos Aires) 9:379–389.

Woodburn, James. 1988. African Hunter-Gatherer Social Organization: Is It Best Understood as a Product of Encapsulation? In *Hunters and Gatherers, vol. 1, History, Evolution, and Social Change*, ed. Tim Ingold, David Riches and James Woodburn, 31–64. Oxford: Berg.

3

⚜ ⚜ —————— ⚜ ⚜

The Morality of the Enxet People of the Paraguayan Chaco and Their Resistance to Assimilation

Stephen W. Kidd

Up to the mid-1960s, and perhaps beyond, social anthropology was dominated by an organismic concept of culture, commonly known as the structural-functionalist approach. Societies were envisaged as harmonious systems, isolated from contact with other societies and, as a result, inherently stable and unchanging. At least, this is how they were represented in the writings of anthropologists through the use of the literary technique known as the ethnographic present. In the words of Eric Wolf (1982), the inhabitants of the non-Western world were regarded as "people without history," as if the global expansion of European culture had left them untouched. This was reflected in the anthropological research undertaken among the peoples of lowland South America, who were frequently described as if they were isolated from contact with the outside world. In fact, given the tendency for anthropologists to make themselves disappear in their own writings, this isolation often seemed absolute.

The reality, however, is different. As anthropologists now readily admit, no culture is static, nor are cultures entirely cut off from the surrounding world. They undergo processes of continual transformation, with one of the greatest influences for change being the spread of Western culture. To many observers, it seems as if the forces of globalization are propelling the cultures of the world toward an ever-increasing and inevitable homogenization. As indigenous American peoples lose their feathers, pull on Western clothes, attend church, become obsessed with soccer, and increasingly participate in the market economy, it would seem that acculturation is a foregone conclusion. Indeed, many people believe that deculturation would be a more accurate description.

This chapter will suggest that there are grounds for greater optimism and that many changes are perhaps more superficial than are often supposed.

Through the study of one Chaco people, it will be shown that certain essential elements of indigenous culture, including those that are key factors in defining indigenous identity, have proved themselves resistant to the forces of assimilation. The aspects of indigenous culture that will be focused on in this chapter are moral values and social relations.

The people in question are the Enxet of the Paraguayan Chaco, who, despite suffering almost a century of colonization, exploitation, and missionary indoctrination, have managed to maintain an authentic indigenous morality that, in turn, continues to exercise a significant influence on how they behave toward each other. Despite the transformed conditions in which they live, especially the penetration of money into their economy and multiple attempts to introduce development projects that are frequently predicated on the contrary values of the marketplace, it will be shown that Enxet social relationships continue to manifest a distinctive character when they are compared to those that are prevalent among the members of the surrounding society.[1]

Yet without land it is difficult for indigenous people to maintain their cultures. Therefore, the Enxet are becoming increasingly involved in politics in an attempt to recover part of their traditional territory. The latter part of the chapter will consider the question of indigenous land in the Chaco and will show that despite favorable legislation, government policy is directed toward maintaining the status quo and ignoring indigenous rights.

THE BACKGROUND

The Enxet, with a present-day population of some 13,000, inhabit a territory encompassing some 50,000 square kilometers. They are one of five members of the Maskoy linguistic family, the others being the Sanapaná, Angaité, Toba-Maskoy, and Kaskiha peoples.[2] It is probable that these groups were formed by different migrations from a common ancestor, each intermarrying with the other indigenous groups with whom they came into contact. Neighboring peoples are the Sanapaná and Angaité to the north, the Nivaclé and Maká to the east, and the Toba to the South.[3]

When the Spanish invaders first arrived in the area of present-day Asunción, the eastern border of the future Paraguayan Chaco was inhabited by the Mbayá, Lengua-Juigade, and Enimagá peoples, who, within a short period, had adopted the horse, which they integrated into their culture. When they eventually entered into full-scale conflict with the Spaniards, their ability as horsemen placed them on equal terms, and as a result, the Spaniards were never able to successfully invade the Chaco.[4] At this time, the Enxet lived far from the Paraguay River toward the Pilcomayo River. It was only in the late eighteenth century, after the equestrian peoples had been decimated by disease and the survivors had migrated north, that the Enxet began their occupation of the western bank of the Paraguay River.

Prior to the invasion and colonization of their land, the Enxet were divided into groups of between 150 and 300 people, occupying territories of up to 2,500 square kilometers. People congregated around territorial leaders known as *wese*, to whom they were joined by ties of kinship and affinity. Such leaders were powerful shamans who were meant to use their supernatural abilities to benefit and protect their followers. They defended their group from the supernatural attacks of their enemies and were also expected to be generous. As a result, early observers noted that it was easy to recognize Enxet leaders because they were the poorest members of the community.

For much of the year, the territorial groups were divided into small communities of between 10 and 70 people that set up camps throughout the territory, permitting a more rational use of the natural resources. The Enxet economy was based essentially on hunting, gathering, and fishing, but whether they should be called hunter-gatherers is a debatable point. In the centuries prior to the invasion and colonization of their land, they had adopted certain domestic animals, especially cattle, sheep, goats, and horses. Reports on the numbers of animals vary: an early observer described one village as "prosperous" that had seventeen cattle, five horses, and forty sheep and goats, while another wrote of a community that possessed five hundred goats and sheep and one hundred horses.[5] Nevertheless, despite the discrepancies, it needs to be recognized that stock rearing was of some significance, although it would seem that animals were butchered only in times of need or during festivals. Small-scale horticulture was another activity, and gardens were usually located at some distance from the village so as to protect them from the attentions of the domestic animals. Normally, and in response to the highly localized nature of Chaco rainfall and the dangers presented by plant-eating insects and certain larger mammals, each family cultivated a number of small gardens spread over a wide area. This could be understood as a means of spreading risk. As with domestic animals, the harvest was usually consumed in times of shortage or during feasts.

Indeed, feasts were a regular occurrence. During the summer, when food was abundantly available, the different communities in the territorial group used to congregate together near a bountiful source of the *algarroba* bean. Such festivals could last for a number of months, during which time the major rites, such as the male and female adult initiation ceremonies, took place. Additionally, there was almost interminable dancing, while alcohol, made from *algarroba* or honey, was consumed in large quantities by the men. Once the food became more scarce, the people would again spread out over the territory in smaller communities.

This way of life, though, was not to last. Although the Enxet managed to maintain their independence until the end of the nineteenth century, unknown to them, in 1825 the Paraguayan government declared that the lands of the Chaco region were to become the property of the state. For many years, this made no difference to the situation on the ground since Paraguay made no attempt to colonize the Chaco, but in 1885, with the intention of repaying its foreign debt, the government began to sell off the region on the London Stock Exchange. Within two years, 115,591 square kilometers had been acquired by sixty foreign business interests.[6]

Gradually, the interest of the new owners in their land increased, and they began to send armed expeditions to explore the area. They also persuaded the British South American Missionary Society to commence work among the Enxet with the aim of pacifying them. The mission was a success, and during the early twentieth century, enormous cattle ranches were established throughout the Enxet territory.[7] By the late 1940s their entire land had been fenced off, and the best water sources had been settled by white people.

The colonization of their land had damaging consequences for the Enxet. Their population was devastated by contact with previously unknown diseases and fell to a quarter of its preinvasion number. Their freedom of movement was severely reduced as they were obliged to form more stable settlements on the ranches, in the vicinity of the houses of the owners, and their white employees. Hunting was made subject to permission from the ranch owners and, given the greater size and more stable nature of the communities, the density of the fauna within easy range of the villages was reduced. The men were obliged to provide cheap labor for the ranches, often being paid little more than provisions, cheap clothes, and alcohol.[8] Their domestic animals disappeared, being either consumed to fend off hunger or appropriated by the landowners. Gardening also became increasingly precarious because of the presence of large numbers of cattle.

The main focus of this chapter is on the Enxet living in the zone of influence of the Anglican Mission, which is bounded to the east by the Paraguay River, to the north by the Riacho Gonzalez, and to the south by the Río Montelindo and stretches 200 kilometers to the west. In the mid-1970s the Enxet approached the Anglicans to ask for their support in obtaining land for their permanent settlement. Between 1980 and 1985 the Anglicans were instrumental in purchasing a further 41,000 hectares, in three different areas, for the settlement of the Enxet, Sanapaná, and Angaité, and this was added to the 3,739 hectares they already possessed in the mission station of Makthlawaiya. By the early 1990s there were 3,400 indigenous people resident on the four indigenous colonies of Makthlawaiya, El Estribo, Sombrero Pirí, and La Patria.[9] They comprised 60 to 70 percent of the indigenous population of the area, with the remainder continuing to live on the ranches.

Evidently, the Enxet have undergone major transformations since the beginning of the twentieth century. They control less than 3 percent of their "traditional" territory and have suffered from tremendous exploitation at the hands of the white colonists. Superficially, they seem to have adopted many elements of Western culture, yet a closer examination reveals the continuation of a distinctive indigenous culture that, despite the best efforts of missionaries and the government, remains the dominant influence on their daily lives. Of crucial importance is the persistence of certain moral values, and the next section will demonstrate how these values continue to influence the social and economic relationships of the Enxet.

THE MORAL ECONOMY

To illustrate the nature of daily interpersonal relations, I will focus on one community, the colony of El Estribo, which is located 370 kilometers to the north of Asunción on the southern edge of the Mennonite colonies. Since 1927 the Mennonites, who have a present-day population of some 12,000, have acquired more than 11,000 square kilometers that have become a major focus of economic activity in the Chaco, attracting indigenous people in search of work from all over the region. This has provided the Mennonites with a bountiful supply of cheap labor.

El Estribo was originally settled in 1985 by a group of Enxet attracted by the relatively large areas of sandy soil that appeared eminently suitable for agriculture and by the proximity of the Mennonite labor market. By 1996, 1,300 people resided in the colony, which comprises 9,474 hectares. In the context of the Chaco, El Estribo is considered to be extremely overpopulated. Paraguayan law stipulates that the size of indigenous colonies must be calculated on the basis of a minimum of 100 hectares per family, and experts estimate that 200 hectares per family would be a realistic requirement. Yet in El Estribo, there are only 28 hectares per family, and the situation is exacerbated by the presence of three other Enxet colonies, managed by Mennonites, bordering El Estribo with a further population of 1,700 on 16,000 hectares. In 1992 the Anglican church transferred the land title of El Estribo to the community.

The community is divided into eight different villages that are formed on the basis of groupings of kin and affines. Households often comprise three generations since, after marriage, the son-in-law usually moves in with his parents-in-law. Nevertheless, when the children of a young couple are of school age, they can build separate houses near the wife's parents. Houses within the villages are usually no more than one hundred meters apart, and each household generally has between one and three hectares of land available for gardening.

As we have seen, during the preinvasion period, the Enxet practiced a variety of subsistence activities, and a similar diversified economy continues to be implemented in El Estribo, although the stress given to the different activities is somewhat different. Contemporary alternatives include hunting, fishing, gathering, agriculture, honey production, stock raising, and employment. I will briefly describe each one.

When the Enxet first arrived in El Estribo, there seemed to be an abundance of wild animals. Yet within a short time, their enthusiasm for the hunt had caused such a rapid reduction in the animal population that hunting became an occasional activity of a minority of people. Nowadays, only small prey is caught, such as armadillos and iguanas. These are hunted by individuals or, at most, two men using dogs as trackers. Occasionally, larger groups may be formed for bird hunts: for example, if a large number of waterfowl are spotted nesting in a specific area, a group of men can hunt them at night. They use torches that they suddenly switch on to disorient the birds, which are then easily killed with sticks. A small income can be obtained from the sale of iguana skins.

Fishing is another activity that is rarely practiced in El Estribo. Although it is still common in the east of the region where there are larger bodies of water, El Estribo is located in a relatively dry area and possesses no permanent sources of water, except for a number of large water holes excavated by the Anglicans to provide drinking water.[10] During the wet season, though, a number of shallow lagoons and old river channels fill with water, permitting some temporary fishing, the most popular being for eels that live in mud and are killed by harpoons. Unfortunately, such sources are usually exhausted within a few days. Women, however, occasionally fish in the water holes with line and hooks, but they rarely catch more than two or three small fish.

Gathering is also of limited importance. In part, this is because of the competition of Western foodstuffs that, when there is money, are easily acquired and require minimal preparation. However, it also reflects the lack of natural resources in El Estribo. Palm hearts, which further east are part of the staple diet of the Enxet, are not available in El Estribo, and the situation is similar with many other plant foods. The *algarroba* and *antawa* beans are only available for a short period during the middle of the summer. They are harvested by the women, but only in relatively small quantities since both require considerable preparation. *Algarroba* beans are made into a flour by pounding them with a pestle and mortar and can be stored for up to three months. *Antawa* must be cooked for up to twelve hours, with three or four changes of water, so as to remove a poison. To many women, it seems much easier to buy a kilogram of rice.

Most households cultivate small gardens of up to one hectare in size, although this varies from year to year depending on the availability of the tractor. El Estribo possesses one tractor that, when it is working, is used by the members of the community for their gardens, although they have to pay for its hire. Unfortunately, when the tractor breaks down, it may take months to repair, and if this coincides with the planting season, the gardens can end up being extremely small. There is no alternative form of traction, and most people are unwilling to work their land with a spade. Both men and women cultivate the gardens, although the women have a greater responsibility for weeding and harvesting.

There are always some people in El Estribo who plant cotton as a cash crop. For example, in 1995/96 two villages planted a total of over sixty hectares, with between a half and three hectares of cotton per household.

However, cotton, as with all forms of agriculture in the Chaco, is a risky enterprise due to the unpredictability of the rainfall and the dangers of pest damage. Although the plots are well tended, yields are low when compared to the man-hours invested. In 1995/96 the most successful farmer earned less than U.S. $1,000, which works out to slightly more than U.S. $80 per month. This was significantly more than most people earn and can be compared with the minimum wage of U.S. $220 per month, which is, in itself, regarded as extremely inadequate. The costs of cultivation are usually covered by credits obtained from the local Mennonites.

Approximately 10 percent of adult men and a few women own between one and ten beehives each. These were obtained from the Anglican church on credit and have been relatively successful. Once established, the hives require minimal inputs of labor, and an average hive can produce, in one year, thirty liters of honey that can be sold for U.S. $90. Indeed, for a fraction of the effort, two beehives provide the same income as a hectare of cotton.[11]

There are small numbers of domestic animals in El Estribo. In early 1996, 12 people possessed a total of 41 cattle, there were 14 sheep belonging to 3 people, 2 people had a total of 25 goats, and each household maintained a small number of poultry. This represented a tremendous reduction from 1987, when the Anglican church had given 800 cattle to El Estribo.[12] The cattle were distributed among the adult males of the colony, who each received 1 or 2. Their numbers fell rapidly for a variety of reasons: many were eaten or sold, others died in a drought, while some people who had kept and, indeed, multiplied their animals lost many of them through sickness. Those who still possess cattle maintain more or less a consistent number, selling an animal every year or two.

However, the main innovation in economic activities, when compared with the preinvasion period, is the introduction of waged labor. At any given time, the majority of the inhabitants of El Estribo are outside the colony working for Mennonites or on the ranches to the southeast. In multiple households, though, it is rare for everyone to leave, and the older generation will often stay behind to care for the houses and gardens. This permanent migration has the advantage of reducing the strain on El Estribo's resources and also provides an additional source of income for those left behind since workers often send money to their parents and parents-in-law. Nevertheless, salaries are low, rarely passing U.S. $140 per month, or 65 percent of the minimum wage. Furthermore, although employers are legally obliged to provide their workers with free rations, this rarely happens. As a result, a large proportion of the wage is handed over in the form of provisions, with the cost being deducted at the end of the month. Consequently, the cash received in hand is much less than the nominal wage. Indeed, on some ranches, the workers have their entire wages deducted. Within El Estribo, there are also twelve young men who are employed by the state as teachers and auxiliary nurses earning, on average, U.S. $250 per month.

Therefore, within each household, income and subsistence are obtained from a range of activities that become available at frequent intervals and at different times of the year. People are not dependent on one activity, such as farming, which would provide its harvest during a limited period of the year and would then require storage or the saving of any income from its sale. Such a diversified economy fits in with the vagaries of the Chaco climate and labor market, because it is impossible to predict when a resource will be available or when someone will have a job; multiple activities and alternatives mean that the risk is spread. Furthermore, the diversified economy also dovetails with the character of Enxet economic relations, in which accumulation is shunned and incomes and other yields are used almost immediately.

This refusal to accumulate can be observed in many spheres of life. Within a community, there is a remarkable degree of homogeneity between households in terms of their material possessions. Although people may not be absolutely equal, there are minimal differences between the richest and the poorest. Food is not stored with the aim of consuming it through the leaner winter months, and nobody ever saves money. Even the numbers of domestic animals are kept small, and throughout the whole of the area of influence of the Anglican Mission, I have not met an Enxet who managed to consistently maintain more than twenty cattle.

The egalitarian character of Enxet life is, to a great extent, the result of certain moral values persisting since preinvasion times. The Enxet have a pronounced egalitarian ethic that they express in a number of ways. They frequently refer to themselves as "people without things," a term that is commonly used by Chaco peoples and can be understood as an expression of the Enxet's image of themselves as all equal or, rather, all equally poor.[13] Furthermore, the term used to describe fellow community members is a composite word derived from the terms "equal" and "one." It encapsulates the assumption that those who live together should, ideally, be kin but also alludes to the requirement of economic equality between coresidents. Similarly, calling someone "the same as others" is a great compliment, while "being different" is frequently used as a criticism. People are continually exhorted not to be "above" others.

Another important and related value is the requirement to "love" others. Indeed, the dichotomy of love and hate is a theme around which a great deal of Enxet moral discourse is constructed. Love is intimately associated with giving and generosity so that those who give, love, and those who love, give. Hate, in contrast, is, in normal Enxet discourse, consistently associated with anger, an emotion that should be energetically avoided. Calling someone "angry" is regarded as a severe criticism and is a strong moral judgment on that person's character. People who become visibly angry will often, because of the shame they feel, abandon a community for a period of time.

Both the egalitarian ethic and the requirement to love continue to exercise a powerful influence on the present-day economic relations of the Enxet. To demonstrate this more clearly, I will describe different aspects of the economic relations within contemporary Enxet communities, highlighting their correspondence with these moral values. It should, however, be pointed out that the character of economic relations varies according to the type of property under consideration: food, nonconsumables, domestic animals, and money.

Within households, a dominant theme is love between close kin. All food that enters the household is pooled, and all members have free access to it. Usually, people eat from one pot, although food that can be consumed raw is eaten by anyone at any time. If visitors are in the house, they are treated as members, receiving food whenever people eat. It is within the household that children are raised, and this is described by the Enxet as "caring for them" or "making them grow." This is one aspect of love, and children who seem to be abandoned are looked on with pity and referred to as "those with no one to love them," which is another way of saying that there is no one to give them food. Personal nonconsumable property is regarded as belonging to individuals, but within the household, it is freely lent and borrowed, often without having to ask permission. Indeed, outside observers often fail to identify this element of personal ownership within households since people's use of objects can give the impression that they belong to the family.

Between households, there is a great deal of voluntary sharing of food. This is regarded as an expression of love between people and usually takes place among close kin. Most voluntary sharing is carried out by the women of the household, who are often observed carrying small bundles of food to their parents, children, siblings, and others they regard as close kin. This usually only happens when a household has an excess of food; for example, if a large animal has been killed, and rather than storing it, people prefer to share it out. Within communities, it is often possible to identify closely related households by searching for houses linked by well-trodden paths. Visitors to a house are, on leaving, frequently given food to take with them. In El Estribo, this usually occurs when there is abundant food in the gardens. It is not uncommon to see people returning home weighed down with sacks of watermelons, sweet potatoes, and pumpkins.

People can also give away nonconsumable property as an expression of love. For example, a carpenter in Makthlawaiya received a rare visit from an aunt and her family who lived 150 kilometers away. On their return home, he gave them a table and most of his chairs. When I asked him why, he replied that he had felt sorry for them because they had very little furniture of their own, and anyway, he could make himself more. Personal property can also be voluntarily loaned to others: for example, visitors may be given the use of bicycles to return home.

Much of the literature on hunter-gatherers explains this type of sharing by reference to its economic rationality. If, in times of abundance, a household shares its surplus with others, when it is in need, it will be able to make a claim on the goods of those who are in its debt. Yet while explanations of sharing that emphasize its adaptive nature are certainly appealing, they can be questioned. For example, they can fail to give sufficient attention to the nonreciprocal nature of sharing in indigenous communities, because some households are usually net givers while others are net receivers. An alternative approach has been suggested by Gow (1991), who has demonstrated how the giving of food among the Piro people of Peru is a means of creating social relationships. People give food to those with whom they want to create or maintain a relationship. In this way, a community of nurture is created of safe insiders.[14] Among many South American indigenous peoples, kinship is not regarded as derived from the biological act of procreation and birth but rather as maintained through the social act of giving. Kin relations must be continually enacted by the sharing of food. Thus people who do not share with each other, even though they may be biologically related, will not regard each other as kin.[15]

Among the Enxet, a similar situation exists in that the creation of love is synonymous with the creation of social relationships. People give to those they love and, in this way, maintain the relationship between them; by initiating acts of sharing, love is promoted and a new social relationship is created. Usually, sharing takes place between kin, but not exclusively so. Yet when a relationship of sociality exists between nonkin, they will often refer to each other by the generic term for kin, although they do differentiate them from consanguineal kin by calling them "not proper kin."[16] Similarly, biological kin who rarely, if ever, see each other are often described as being "like they were nonkin," essentially because there is no sharing or interaction between the parties and, therefore, no performance of love.

Love, therefore, among the Enxet must be enacted. Ideally, it is characteristic of how relationships should be within a community since, as mentioned, communities are supposed to be comprised of kin. Yet throughout the whole of Enxet territory there is also a wide dispersion of kin, usually caused by people taking spouses from other communities. Such kin usually attempt to maintain relationships either by visiting periodically or by sending gifts. Indeed, whenever I traveled between Enxet communities, I was frequently asked to carry small gifts from one person to another.

However, not all sharing is done at the initiative of the giver. The Enxet have a term, *nenmagkaxno*, that refers to the action of people visiting others to ask for food. This can be classified as demand sharing, and such a request is almost never refused. It can produce two types of response in the potential giver. If the giver enjoys a close relationship with the person asking, requests are normally responded to happily, and if food is abundant, people may even insist on giving more than has been asked for. In contrast, if the relationship between the two people is not particularly close, the request may provoke resentment in the giver, especially if his food stocks are dwindling. In this case, almost the only way to avoid giving is to lie and say that there is no food. Alternatively, people can hand over some food but ensure that it is of poor quality, such as small sour watermelons.

An examination of the early literature suggests that demand sharing is more prevalent now than it was in precolonial times. Communities then were smaller and comprised groups of closer kin, and it seems that voluntary sharing was much more common. For example, an early missionary reported in 1895 how the different families in a community would share cooked food with each other irrespective of whether the other families already had some or not. Contemporary communities are generally much larger, and it is not possible for one family to voluntarily give to all the other families. Furthermore, some households may not be closely related and may have no real desire to develop closer ties.

Those who practice demand sharing often address potential givers by kin terms, thus, by implication, invoking the requirement to love. Therefore, an open refusal to give would be a denial of kinship and love and could provoke bad feelings. Yet there are also signs of the egalitarian ethic at play. Although the Enxet possess a strong discourse on egalitarianism, it should not be assumed that everyone voluntarily strives to be equal. Many people are ambitious and greedy and can try to keep their produce for themselves and their household. Demand sharing is one means at the disposal of the community to inhibit accumulation by others and could be conceived of as a type of levelling mechanism that ensures that community members remain equal.[17]

Nonconsumable possessions are not as susceptible to demand sharing as food since they are individually owned and much more closely tied to the person of the owner. They cannot easily be alienated, and as a result, requests to give are rare. Much more usual are requests to borrow nonconsumables such as bicycles, rifles, and tools. The verb employed for borrowing is "to use." Since borrowing does not imply alienation, people are much less reticent about practicing it. Such requests are not easily refused, but once borrowed objects are handed over, they may not be returned for a long time. Often, the owner himself will have to visit the borrower's house to ask for the object's return. Furthermore, there is no guarantee that borrowed objects will be taken care of, and they are often returned in a state of disrepair. For example, one man in El Estribo lent a drill to his brother-in-law, who lived only three hundred meters away. After waiting over a year for its return, he eventually visited his brother-in-law's house to ask for it back. Unfortunately, it had been left outside the house, and the handle had been broken by the children. The brother-in-law offered no compensation, and the owner could not bring himself to ask. Nevertheless, he complained about what had happened for days, but always out of earshot of his brother-in-law.

Being able to borrow more valuable objects is one means of ensuring that the owner is obliged to share them with the wider community. Furthermore, the fact that they are often broken when in the care of borrowers means that owners are unlikely to keep objects for long. Some people can tire of the constant demands to borrow their possessions and decide to sell them and in that way avoid the problem. As a result, any inequality caused by someone's possession of a more valuable object evidently lasts only for a limited period.

Indeed, whenever incipient hierarchies arise, the egalitarian ethic comes into play. An illustrative example occurred in the colony of Makthlawaiya. Over a period of years, one of the leaders rented out a corral to neighboring ranchers that they used to load their cattle into lorries when sending them to market. Through this, he obtained substantial sums of money, most of which he kept for himself. This caused much ill-feeling since the other members of the community believed that the income generated should be shared between everyone. Their constant appeals made no impression on the leader, so when the leader was temporarily absent from the community, some of the men dismantled the corral and sold the wood to a local trader. On his return, the leader discovered a fait accompli about which he could do nothing. Some days later, those involved explained to me that they had done it because of the leader's refusal to share. They believed that it would be fairer for no one to receive anything than for one person to retain a monopoly.

THE CHALLENGE OF MONEY

With the colonization of their land, the Enxet have inexorably been drawn into the market economy and, apparently, into a set of economic rules and practices that would seem to contrast sharply with their sharing economy. Perhaps the greatest challenge has been the penetration of money into their internal economy. Indeed, many anthropologists have suggested that it is money that poses one of the greatest threats to the egalitarian system of social relations among indigenous American peoples.[18] They have pointed out that money is qualitatively different from other consumable and nonconsumable possessions in that it is an impersonal quantitative ratio that enables property in one form to be easily converted into property in any other form.[19] It is believed that on entering an indigenous economy, money will inevitably lead to the creation of depersonalized market relations between people and the eventual disappearance of sharing and gift giving, which are, as I have shown, constitutive of love and social relationships among the Enxet. It is suggested that people will begin to accumulate, and hierarchies will gradually appear within the formerly egalitarian societies. It is as if money were seen as a deadly virus among indigenous peoples, a powerful and anonymous force that destroys any system with which it comes into contact.

Yet the Enxet response to money hints at a greater cultural resilience and suggests that their moral values have greatly influenced the market economy's intrusion into their communities. Although many people have access to money, it is neither accumulated nor particularly effective in creating the anonymous relationships of the marketplace. Of course, in many cases, the transformative potential of money is reduced as a result of the small pro-portion of wages that is received as cash. Yet even when much larger sums are obtained, such as with the sale of the cotton harvest or in higher wages such as those of the teachers, its effect on social relations is minimal. The Enxet exhibit what Hugh-Jones (1992:64) describes as a "windfall mental-ity." He gives the example of the Barasana of the northwest Amazon, who believe that manufactured goods are imbued with a special power that makes them irresistibly attractive and that leads them to spend their money uncontrollably. Although I have not heard this explanation among the Enxet, they do seem to behave in a similar way. The Enxet teachers, who have to travel to Asunción to collect their wages, are capable of almost ex-hausting them within a couple of days, often returning to their communities with very little cash. This could also be partly due to their awareness that on returning to their community, a number of people will ask for loans that may or may not be repaid. By using up their money, they avoid such re-quests. Alternatively, on returning to the community, those with cash will often use it to bet on football matches or in gambling. They can also be en-couraged to buy large quantities of alcohol that the drinkers in the commu-nity are happy to help consume.[20] Such levelling mechanisms maintain equality within the community.

Money can also be constitutive of love. Sons and sons-in-law who are away working will often send up to a quarter of their wages back to their parents or parents-in-law every month. Money can also be used as a gift, and I have frequently been asked to carry money between relatives in differ-ent communities. Individuals with access to money often buy objects that will be used by a wider group of people. For example, if a soccer team needs a set of shirts, instead of the members of the team pooling their resources, an individual with money will buy the shirts for everyone. Indeed, it needs to be recognized that the ease with which money is converted into another object facilitates its being shared. If it is used to buy food, it enters the household's pool of food and can be shared in the normal way. Nonconsumables can also be purchased and used as gifts.

Even when people within a community employ each other, the relation-ship between employer and employee does not lead to a breakdown in social relations, nor should it be seen as tantamount to coercion, as suggested by a number of writers.[21] In El Estribo, most employment occurs during the cot-ton harvest, when the Enxet cultivators pay occasional laborers for each kilogram of cotton harvested. Such employment is purely voluntary, and the wages compare favorably with those on offer from local Mennonite farmers. Indeed, the harvests of most gardens are so small, rarely passing a thousand kilograms, that it would be possible for the majority of households to har-vest their own cotton by themselves. This suggests that the employment of laborers, who are often kin, is a means of distributing the benefits of the har-vest. Furthermore, it is not possible to isolate the relations between employer and employee from the encompassing social event: the employee receives food and drink from his host, and friendly banter between the parties is common, all of which are constitutive of social relationships.

LAND AS COMMON PROPERTY

Therefore, even within the modern colonial context, economic relations among the Enxet continue to be influenced by an adherence to key moral values. Yet it is important to recognize the significant role played by the land-tenure system in underpinning these relations. Prior to the invasion of their territory, no individual maintained exclusive rights to any area of land or natural resources. Access was open to everyone, and people from one territory were able to hunt in the territories of other groups. Consequently, no one could use land as a basis for wealth creation and as a means of coercing others. In contrast, the land-tenure system functioned as a major impediment to the development of hierarchies and inequalities.[22]

Such a land-tenure system has continued to the present day. The Paraguayan Constitution states that indigenous land titles should be held in common by all the members of the community, and although the leaders sign the title deed, they only do so as representatives of the community. In 1990 the community of El Estribo designated four people to be its official leaders. These leaders are well aware that although their names figure on the land title, they have no more rights than anyone else. If they were to abuse their position, it is almost certain that the community would remove them as leaders, as has happened in a number of other colonies.

The only rights of exclusion in El Estribo are to the garden plots, but these are only the right of use and may be forfeited if people abandon their house for an extended period. The vast majority of the land in El Estribo is open to everyone, although this has frequently been a source of conflict, especially over the use of the colony's timber resources. Problems can be caused by outsiders approaching individual members of the colony in an attempt to purchase timber, especially a tree called *palo santo* that is used by the Mennonites for fence posts. Armed with axes and occasionally with chain saws, individuals or small groups of people can unilaterally begin cutting down the trees. The community finds it extremely difficult to respond to such actions since prohibiting individuals from using the natural resources is anathema to them. In the early years of El Estribo, when the timber resources appeared to the new settlers to be limitless, they found that the easiest response was for everyone to join in the extraction and obtain short-term profits from the sale of the timber.[23] Indeed, at this time, the timber cutting was stopped only by a combination of the intervention of Anglican missionaries, the availability of short-term work on Mennonite farms, and a gradual realization that the forest resources were being significantly depleted.

Since then, the people's awareness that the *palo santo* is in danger of being totally exhausted has brought a change of attitude. At various times, in community meetings, it has been decided that the wood should only be cut down in small quantities and for specific purposes that would be of benefit to the whole community. Yet on occasions, individuals, encouraged by local Mennonites, continue to unilaterally extract timber. Stopping them is dependent on someone being willing to take the initiative to confront them. This is not easy since the Enxet actively avoid conflict, which could easily be misinterpreted as anger and hatred, and so the speed of response varies greatly. Most people justify their nonintervention by stating that the responsibility for taking action lies with the leaders, although they themselves would prefer not to have this role. In some cases, when the individual concerned is not regarded as a particularly strong character, the leaders can deal with the matter relatively quickly, but with strong individuals, weeks may pass before effective action is taken, and in any case, the guilty parties are never punished. The most that can be hoped for is that they agree to desist.

However, despite the problems caused by the land-tenure system within the present-day context of limited resources, the fact that no one can exercise exclusive, long-term control over the land is a key factor in limiting the possibilities for the development of hierarchies. Rather than working against Enxet moral values, open access to land contributes significantly to their continuing efficacy and significance.

THE THREAT OF DEVELOPMENT PROJECTS TO INDIGENOUS MORALITY

It is clear that the Anglican church's land-acquisition program was seriously inadequate and resulted in severe overpopulation in the indigenous colonies. Yet the mission was determined to ensure the long-term settlement of the Enxet and, realizing that the traditional indigenous economy was not feasible on the small areas of land acquired, decided to complement their land purchases with the implementation of economic development projects. The missionaries firmly believed that agriculture should provide the basis of the indigenous economy in the colonies and were convinced that to be successful, they would have to actively promote a transformation of Enxet culture. They recognized that an exclusively agricultural economy would demand the demise of the indigenous practice of sharing. In its place, they sought to encourage accumulation so that each family would be responsible for its own destiny. Evidently, this would present a formidable challenge to the Enxet egalitarian ethic and the requirement to love.

Although it is not my intention to present an overall critique of the impact of development projects on the Enxet, I am concerned with highlighting the role played by Enxet moral values in ensuring the failure of almost all the projects attempted by the Anglicans. As will be demonstrated, the Enxet transform development projects so that, rather than encouraging cultural change, they are made to correspond to Enxet values and practices.[24]

One of the largest projects implemented by the Anglican church was cotton production. The specific project to be examined was undertaken in the early 1980s in the colony of Sombrero Pirí and was divided into four stages: the initial land preparation and planting; the care of the crop through weeding and the spraying of insecticide; the harvest; and the saving of any income to enable a family to survive until the next harvest. The first three stages required an investment of both labor and money, while the fourth stage was dependent on the principle of accumulation and nonsharing. Yet those who settled in Sombrero Pirí in 1980 were essentially penniless. Consequently, the initial plowing of the land, purchasing of the seed, and sowing were provided on credit from the Anglican church. The Enxet were then faced with having to survive until the sale of the harvest, during which time they would also have to maintain the crop free of weeds. They decided to present the Anglicans with a choice: either they were to be provided with rations, or else they would abandon their fields and look for work elsewhere. The missionaries responded by giving the cotton cultivators food on credit, thereby enabling them to remain in the colony until the harvest. Further credit covered the cost of insecticides. By the time of the harvest, each cultivator was faced with a debt to the church that was greater than any income that would be received from the sale of the cotton. It was clear to them that investing their labor in harvesting their own crop was worthless, and so, just as the harvest was about to commence, many people abandoned their gardens and traveled north to harvest cotton for the Mennonites. The missionaries were powerless to stop them, and it was only when the Mennonite cotton harvest had finished that the indigenous people returned to Sombrero Pirí. The debts could not be recovered, and after a couple of years, the Anglicans eventually decided to write them off.

In this way, the Enxet of Sombrero Pirí successfully managed to transform a cotton project predicated on the principle of accumulation into a means of obtaining immediate and consistent returns that could be consumed and distributed according to Enxet values. They rejected the missionaries' invocations to accumulate and save and, instead, ensured that the project did not present a threat to their egalitarian social relations.

It is interesting to note the means by which the indigenous people were able to manipulate the missionaries throughout the course of the project. They managed to convince them that weeding would be impossible without rations, yet some years later, the Enxet of El Estribo demonstrated that this was not true. Cultivating cotton on their own initiative, the El Estribo people maintained their plots clear of weeds by taking advantage of their diversified economy. Some members of the households left the colony in search of work and sent back food and money to help those who had remained behind, who, in addition, also hunted, fished, and gathered whenever the opportunity presented itself. They also obtained some income from the sale of honey and grew their own food in their gardens, although it should be recognized that very occasionally, they did receive a small supplement of free rations from politicians interested in winning their vote.

The people in Sombrero Pirí preferred to take advantage of the missionaries' sentiments. Given that the missionaries were most enthusiastic about the success of the cotton project, having had the initial idea and having received financial support for the project from abroad that would eventually have to be accounted for, when it seemed as if the project would fail, they were unwilling to admit defeat and promptly agreed to provide the desired rations. At a deeper level, they were also worried about antagonizing the Enxet and driving them away from their allegiance to the Anglican church. Indeed, throughout the history of the Anglican Mission in Paraguay, economic enticements had consistently and explicitly been used to attract the Enxet to the church. Additionally, individual missionaries were reluctant to become unpopular with the Enxet and so, at times, were willing to accede to requests that should perhaps have been rejected. For the same reasons, when the cotton cultivators refused to pay their debts, the Anglicans avoided pressing them too hard and, eventually, decided that it would be less damaging to wipe the slate clean. Indeed, so clean was it wiped that within a short time further opportunities for credit were being offered to the same people.[25]

For their part, the Enxet feel that if they are to follow the Anglican church, the missionaries must respond by demonstrating love. Since love and gift giving are conceptually linked, the Enxet feel that it is entirely legitimate for them to receive material goods from the missionaries. They envisage the missionaries in terms of the traditional leader, the *wese*, who was meant to love and care for his people and, in consequence, was expected to be generous. Missionaries are also referred to as *wese*, and it is not surprising that the same expectations of generosity are made of them. If such generosity is not forthcoming, the indigenous people are quite willing to find another *wese* to follow. In the Chaco, shifts in the denominational allegiance of indigenous people are quite common.[26]

Interestingly, the term *wese* is no longer employed to refer to contemporary indigenous leaders. They are called *akkemhapmomye*, meaning "he who stands in front." Despite the name change, they are still expected to care for and be generous to their people. Given the prevailing conditions, this is impossible to achieve by means of their own production. One alternative is for leaders to obtain large quantities of goods from outside agents that can then be distributed among the members of the community. In the context of development projects, it is usually the indigenous leaders who negotiate with the missionaries about any extra benefits, as happened with the rations in Sombrero Piri. However, since the advent in 1989 of a democratic political system in Paraguay, the competing political parties have become a particularly fecund source of goods. The leaders of El Estribo often travel to the capital city of Asunción with the aim of offering their community's vote in exchange for some form of material benefit. The most common goods on offer are provisions that the politicians often illegally divert from projects for other sectors of the population. As the elections approach, the frequency with which provisions are sent to the indigenous communities increases. On arrival, they are unloaded at the house of the leader, who is then responsible for ensuring their distribution. Community members congregate around his house, and the load is carefully divided up, with families receiving as much as twenty-five kilograms of food each. In this way, the leader is able to show his utility and his ability to care for his people.

THE ENXET STRUGGLE TO RECOVER THEIR LAND

Although the Enxet have shown a desire to resist being assimilated into Western culture by retaining key moral values and social practices, this does not alter the fact that the contemporary structural conditions in the Chaco hold them in a permanently disadvantageous situation vis-à-vis the national society. Of the many difficulties they face, it is their lack of access to land that is the most critical. As I have shown for El Estribo, the small area of land that they have at their disposal is insufficient for their needs, and this situation is repeated throughout the Paraguayan Chaco. Indeed, over 80 percent of indigenous colonies have less than the minimum area of 100 hectares per family that is demanded by law.

This situation is in direct contravention of the Paraguayan Constitution, which states that "the indigenous peoples have the right to land held as common property, of sufficient size and quality for the conservation and development of their particular lifestyles." This would suggest that each indigenous people should have enough land to permit hunting, gathering, and fishing. This would, given the ecological conditions of the Chaco, require significantly more than 100 hectares per family. To put things in perspective, it is probable that the community of El Estribo has a land deficit of more than 60,000 hectares.

There is also the question of justice. The indigenous peoples of the Chaco were, until recently, the de facto undisputed owners of the region, even if this ownership was not formalized in written documents. At no time have they received compensation for the land they lost, nor have they signed any treaties that would have extinguished their rights to their territories. The legitimacy of their rights was acknowledged by the Paraguayan state when it ratified Convention 169 of the International Labor Organization in 1993. This treaty is the most significant piece of international legislation dealing with the rights of indigenous peoples and states that "the rights of ownership and possession of the peoples concerned over the lands which they traditionally occupy shall be recognised." If this legislation were to be fully implemented, extensive areas of the Chaco would have to be titled to the indigenous people.

Yet despite the strength and clarity of the existing legislation, the Paraguayan government has shown little inclination to ensure its implementation. There exists a complete lack of political will, which is not surprising given the close links of the government to the rich landowners of the Chaco. The response of the Enxet has been to initiate a series of land claims. Between 1989 and 1996, fifteen communities presented claims for a total of 185,000 hectares. Most were by those still without land, but two existing colonies, El Estribo and Makthlawaiya, requested amplifications of 13,000 hectares and 20,000 hectares, respectively.

The justification that the Enxet give for their land claims can be discerned in their discourse on the past and reflect the two perspectives highlighted in the legislation: the need for justice and the practical requirements of the indigenous people. However, such historical accounts should not be seen as true and objective narratives of past events. Rather, the Enxet actively re-imagine their past as a means of interpreting their present precarious situation and justifying their political actions.

With regard to the question of justice, the Enxet describe how they used to be the only inhabitants of their territory and how they defended it from Paraguayan invasion. The following is an account that is commonly narrated:

A long time ago, a large number of Paraguayan soldiers entered the Chaco. When the shamans first saw them, they said to themselves, "These Paraguayans are really unfortunate because they have no power." So the shamans sent wasps to attack them, and the soldiers fled out of the Chaco. However, some time later they returned, and this time the shamans used their power to give them severe cramps in their legs. The Enxet were able to approach the soldiers and kill them by smashing their heads with clubs. One was saved and his ear was cut off. He was sent back across the river and ordered to tell the rest of the Paraguayans that they were never to return.

If our concern were with "true" facts, it would have to be admitted that this story has little objective basis since, prior to the colonization of the Chaco, there were only minor skirmishes between Paraguayans and Enxet. Yet it is an important story for the Enxet in that it demonstrates to them that they defended their land from Paraguayan invaders. This image is associated with other stories that describe how the only inhabitants of the Chaco used to be indigenous people. For example, one Enxet described in a written history the following account.

In the past there were no patrons in the Chaco. It was the land of the Enxet, and there was no need for them to work. They could always travel freely to other places, wherever they felt like going. If they saw fish in a lake, they were able to go there [to fish] because they did not have any work and there were no patrons in the Chaco. It was only Enxet who lived in the Chaco, and they were not worried about anything. They were only afraid of wild animals such as tigers, *tamayawhan*,[27] or other things that had spiritual power. (Aníbal Lopez 1996:23)

The conviction, as represented in Enxet history, that they used to be the only inhabitants of their land and that they fought to keep it provides a powerful justification, at least to themselves, of their land claims. Indeed, it may be that the development of these histories has, in part, been related to the land campaign.

Other narratives stress their practical need for more land. For example:

A long time ago, the mission was the owner of the whole area.[28] At that time there were no Paraguayans in the Chaco. The missionaries then called their compatriots— Gosling, Kent, Kennedy, Gustafson, Gray, amd others—and told each one that they could have the land located around different Enxet villages. They did not buy the land, but each one was told that it was his job to look after the Enxet on his land. They did that, and in turn, the Enxet worked for them helping them, to establish their ranches. However, the children of these original owners forgot what they were told by the missionaries and began to mistreat the Enxet.

Although this account has little historical basis, since the Anglican missionaries were never the owners of the Chaco, it does reflect the perspective of the Enxet. It contrasts the early period of colonization, during which they were still allowed to hunt while receiving employment on the ranches, with the contemporary situation, which is characterized by restrictions on hunting and poor working conditions. The Enxet sense of well-being has diminished, and they recognize that the only way to improve their living conditions is to obtain more land.

In response to the government's inaction regarding the land claims, since 1993 the Enxet, with the support of nonindigenous sympathizers, have become politically much more active. Enxet leaders have become prominent in their criticism of the government and the landowners. Many times they have been interviewed in the newspapers and on radio and television and have strongly attacked the government's unwillingness to resolve their claims. Their lawyers have initiated a large number of legal actions against the landowners, including suing for unpaid wages, obtaining injunctions to prohibit deforestation on the lands they are claiming, and ensuring access to ranches for the purpose of hunting. Indeed, in October 1995, four hundred Enxet marched through Asunción to Parliament demanding that resources be set aside in the national budget for the financing of their land claims.

In response to the Enxet campaign, the government has made some changes to its policy. Following the protest march, it promised to budget U.S. $45 million over three years for the purchase of indigenous land. By mid-1997, 35,000 hectares had been acquired for three Enxet communities. Yet this still leaves the vast majority of Enxet claims unresolved, and many seem no closer to a resolution. Indeed, in early 1996 the community of Yesamatathla was expelled from its land by the owner of the ranch on which they lived. Despite numerous appeals, their plight was totally ignored by the government. Furthermore, the availability of money for land purchases has led to a sharp increase in corruption. Land has been bought at prices well above the market value, and the government has even purchased large areas of land that have never been claimed by indigenous communities, again at highly inflated prices. The attorney-general's office has instigated an investigation into the actions of the president of the government institute responsible for the land purchases, but this has made little difference to the situation. The overpricing of land continues, with the result that the budget is wasted and the Enxet fear that their land claims will never be resolved.

CONCLUSION

The Enxet, therefore, are striving to resist the forces of globalization that threaten both their culture and their very well-being. This chapter has highlighted two aspects of this resistance: on the one hand, they are struggling to maintain certain moral values that play a key role in determining the distinctive character of their internal social relations while, on the other, they have begun to participate in the Paraguayan political process in an attempt to have their rights to their lands recognized.

Ensuring the access of indigenous people to their land must be the basis of any attempt to resolve the problems that they are facing. Without adequate land, the Enxet will continue to be obliged to serve as a source of cheap and easily exploited labor. The present colonies are incapable of supporting their inhabitants. Indeed, it may be better to conceive of them as work camps in which the Enxet are kept alive while they are not in employment and where they can be easily found by prospective employers. In this way, the colonies serve the interests of the ranchers and Mennonites, who no longer have to worry about the presence of large numbers of unemployed Enxet on their properties. If the Enxet were to obtain an adequate area of land for their settlement, this would radically transform their present situation. They would benefit from the increase in natural resources that would allow hunting, gathering, and fishing to flourish alongside their other subsistence activities. They would also be faced with the option, rather than the necessity, of looking for employment in white-owned establishments. Their power to negotiate adequate wages would increase substantially since they would possess the viable alternative of returning to their land.

Yet the realization of such a scenario would require a radical change in Paraguayan government policy and would demand of the government a commitment to respect its own Constitution. Unfortunately, this shows little sign of happening. As late as 1995, Paraguay and the European Union signed an agreement to implement a project for the sustainable development of the Chaco. Among other things, the project aims "to civilise" the "primitive" indigenous people of the Chaco and "integrate" them into the national economy. Such ethnocentric language is reminiscent of the nineteenth century and seems totally out of place on the eve of a new millennium. It would suggest a need for the Paraguayan government (and the relevant authorities of the European Union) to reassess their perception of indigenous people. They are neither pristine savages nor deculturated hangers-on to the fringes of Western society. Rather, they must be viewed as a moral people, with rights that must be respected, whose survival as distinctive cultures will play a major contribution in enhancing the community of nations.

NOTES

Research for this chapter was undertaken with the support of the Economic and Social Research Council of the United Kingdom and an Emslie Horniman grant for fieldwork awarded by the Royal Anthropological Institute.

1. Renshaw (1988) also examines the economic morality of the indigenous people of the Paraguayan Chaco.

2. Naming indigenous groups is often fraught with difficulty, and the Enxet are no exception. Until recently, they were usually referred to as the Lengua, but since this term has pejorative connotations in Paraguay, it has gradually been replaced by the term Enxet, the name used by the people themselves. However, the Sanapaná and Angaité also refer to themselves as Enxet, while the Toba-Maskoy call themselves Enenxet.

3. During the late nineteenth century, the Toba-Maskoy were considered to be the northernmost territorial group of the Enxet. It is only during the twentieth century that they have been recognized as a separate people.

4. For more information on conflicts of the indigenous peoples with the Spanish, see Susnik (1981, 1983).

5. Freund (1894:79) and Pride (1901:52).

6. For more information on the land sale, see Laino (1976).

7. Even in 1991, most ranches were larger than 10,000 hectares, and one was over 300,000 hectares.

8. Chase-Sardi (1972:203) provides a vivid description of the working conditions of the Enxet in the 1960s.

9. The title of the mission station of Makthlawaiya was handed over to the Enxet in 1991. La Patria is mainly occupied by Angaité and Sanapaná.

10. Such water holes are about forty meters by twenty meters by two meters in size. Although the water is for drinking, it is unhealthy, especially in the dry season, when the volume of water is reduced considerably.

11. The cotton-production figures that I am making the comparison with are the average for El Estribo in 1995/96, not optimal figures.

12. The Anglicans had managed a ranch on the colonies of Makthlawaiya and Sombrero Pirí that had a total of 3,200 head of cattle in 1987. In that year, as an attempt to break from the paternalistic nature of their work, they handed the cattle over to those Enxet, Sanapaná, and Angaité who were resident in the colonies.

13. See Renshaw (1986:181). This term is not entirely synonymous with our concept of poor, which we, of course, would never use to characterize ourselves as a distinct ethnic group. Indeed, the Enxet possess another word, =yosek, which refers more to poverty in the sense of the suffering caused by it.

14. See also Overing (1993).

15. For more information on views of kinship, see Overing (1989), McCallum (1989), Gow (1991), and Belaunde (1992).

16. The Enxet practice exogamous marriage; that is, they only marry nonkin.

Therefore, if the category of real kin were to be expanded to include all those with whom they have social relationships, they would reduce their marriage possibilities and those of their children. It is possibly for this reason that they maintain a distinction between the general term for kin, which includes all people with whom they have a close social relationship, and the term for real kin, which refers to a biological relationship.

17. See Barnard and Woodburn (1988) for more information on the concept of levelling mechanisms.

18. See, for example, Thomas (1982:239ff.), Renshaw (1986:192), and McCallum (1989:206).

19. For a discussion of the properties of money, see Parry and Bloch (1989) and Peterson (1991).

20. In an explanation reminiscent of the belief of the Barasana, the Enxet say that alcohol possesses a spiritual owner that sings and attracts people to it.

21. See, for example, Thomas (1982:240), Renshaw (1986:208; 1988:346), and McCallum (1989:235).

22. Ingold (1986:233–234) described such a land-tenure system as "sharing in," which he contrasted with "sharing out," a term referring to the sharing of food by households and individuals. He suggested that "sharing out" is underwritten by the positive principle of "sharing in."

23. The concept that natural resources exist in abundance is common to many peoples whose economies are predicated on hunting and gathering.

24. An important structural factor in explaining the failure of development projects is the inadequacy of the Enxet land base. Even if the projects had been exceptionally well designed and executed, the lack of land would have ensured that they could not succeed. However, I will not be dealing with this factor in this section. See also Wallis (1985) for a further discussion of how Chaco peoples transform development projects.

25. A similar project to the one described for Sombrero Pirí was never attempted in El Estribo because, by the time El Estribo was settled, the failure of the cotton projects was apparent. A degree of cynicism had set in among the missionaries, who, from 1984 onwards, actively avoided repeating their experiences in Sombrero Pirí.

26. See, for example, Miller (1971:151).

27. The *tamayawhan* is a hairy spirit that the Enxet nowadays associate with the bear. This spirit eats honey, and it is said that if menstruating women consume honey, they will turn into *tamayawhan*.

28. The area meant by this statement is essentially that within which the Mission worked.

REFERENCES

Barnard, A., and J. Woodburn. 1988. Property, Power, and Ideology in Hunting and Gathering Societies: An Introduction. In *Hunters and Gatherers*, vol. 2: *Property, Power, and Ideology*, ed. Tim Ingold, David Riches, and James Woodburn, 4–31. Explorations in Anthropology. New York and Oxford: Berg.

Belaunde, L. A. 1992. Gender, Commensality, and Community among the Airo-Pai of West Amazonia (Secoya, Western-Tukanoan Speaking). Ph.D. diss., University of London.

Chase-Sardi, M. 1972. The Present Situation of the Indians in Paraguay. In *The Situation of the Indian in South America*, ed. W. Dostal, 173–217. Geneva: World Council of Churches.

Freund, P. A. 1894. Letter to President of Paraguay, 30.12.1893. *The South American Missionary Magazine*, 28:78–79.

Gow, P. 1991. *Of Mixed Blood: Kinship and History in Peruvian Amazonia*. Oxford: Clarendon Press.

Hugh-Jones, S. 1992. Yesterday's Luxuries, Tomorrow's Necessities: Business and Barter in Northwest Amazon. In *Barter, Exchange, and Value: An Anthropological Approach*, ed. C. Humphrey and S. Hugh-Jones, 42–74. Cambridge: Cambridge University Press.

Ingold, T. 1986. *The Appropriation of Nature: Essays on Human Ecology and Social Relations*. Manchester: Manchester University Press.

Laino, D. 1976. *Paraguay: De la independencia a la dependencia (historia del saqueo inglés en el Paraguay de la posguerra)*. Asunción: Ediciones Cerro Cora.

Lopez, Aníbal. 1996. *Aptaxésama egmok apwanyam apwesey Leon Chaves*. Asunción: Tierraviva.

McCallum, C. 1989. Gender, Personhood, and Social Organization amongst the Cashinahua of Western Amazonia. Ph.D. diss., University of London.

Miller, E. S. 1971. The Argentine Toba Evangelical Religious Service. *Ethnology* 10:149–159.

Overing, J. 1989. The Aesthetics of Production: The Sense of Community among the Cubeo and Piaroa. *Dialectical Anthropology* 14:159–175.

———. 1993. The Anarchy and Collectivism of the 'Primitive Other': Marx and Sahlins in the Amazon. In *Socialism*, ed. C. Hann, pp. 43–58. London: Routledge.

Parry, J., and M. Bloch. 1989. Introduction: Money and the Morality of Exchange. In *Money and the Morality of Exchange*, ed. J. Parry and M. Bloch, 1–32. Cambridge: Cambridge University Press.

Peterson, N. 1991. Introduction. In *Cash, Commoditisation and Changing Foragers*, ed. Nicholas Peterson and Toshio Matsuyama, Senri Ethnological Studies 30:1–16. Osaka: National Museum of Ethnology.

Pride, A. 1901. Itineration among Suhin Villages. *South American Missionary Society Annual Report*, 51–57.

Renshaw, J. 1986. The Economy and Economic Morality of the Indians of the Paraguayan Chaco. Ph.D. diss., University of London.

———. 1988. Property, Resources, and Equality among the Indians of the Paraguayan Chaco. *Man* 23:334–352.

Susnik, B. 1981. *Etnohistoria de los Chaqueños, 1650–1910*. Los aborígenes del Paraguay, vol. 3/1. Asunción: Museo Etnográfico "Andrés Barbero."

———. 1983. *El rol de los indígenas en la formación y vivencia del Paraguay*. Vol. 2. Asunción: Instituto Paraguayo de Estudios Nacionales.

Thomas, D. J. 1982. *Order without Government: The Society of the Pemon Indians of Venezuela*. Urbana: University of Illinois Press.

Wallis, C. 1985. *Cuatro proyectos del Chaco*. Holland: Comisión Intereclesiástica de Coordinación para Proyectos de Desarrollo (ICCO).

Wolf, E. R. 1982. *Europe and the People without History*. Berkeley: University of California Press.

4

The *Capitanía* of the Izozo: The Struggle for Political Autonomy among the Guaraní Indians of Eastern Bolivia

Silvia María Hirsch

It was windy, as usual. On my first visit to the Izozo in 1984, the dry, dusty north wind so characteristic of the Chaco covered me with dust when I strolled through the community. I paid a brief visit to the great leader Bonifacio Barrientos, known to his people as *Kuaraia Guasu* (great shadow), who would die a year later. This chief had ruled his people for over fifty years, had met several of Bolivia's presidents, and had struggled to defend the Izoceño-Guaraní people and their territory. I was awed in the presence of this frail man who had once stood to defend his people. By the following year, when I visited the region again, Bonifacio Barrientos had died, and his youngest son, named after him, but known as Boni Chico, was in charge. (See photograph 1.) Deciding the topic of the fieldwork for my future dissertation, I wondered whether such a young and inexperienced man could become the leader of sixteen communities and face many challenges and obstacles. What struck me while visiting the Izozo was the strong presence of the chiefs, the involvement and participation of the Izoceños in development projects, and their struggle to defend their territory and improve their living conditions. The first thing one learned about the Izozo was that the Izoceños maintained their *capitanía*, their traditional political organization, and that they were proud of the struggle of their past leaders.

In 1986 I returned to the Izozo to stay for a year. The first week of my fieldwork, an assembly of *capitanes* (chiefs) took place in the community of La Brecha. This meeting was organized to discuss future development projects that would be implemented in the region, and I as a young graduate student had to ask the permission of this assembly to conduct my research in the area. To me, these events synthesized the powerful role of the political

1. The *mburuvisa guasu*, Boni Chico (right), the anthropologist (center), and an advisor to the *capitanía* (left) in front of the *mburuvisa*'s office in the Izozo in 1996

organization, the enduring legacy of the chiefs, and the strong sense of autonomy among the Izoceños.[1]

The Izoceño-Guaraní Indians of eastern Bolivia (map 4) are known throughout the country for their political struggles, their ability to secure their land titles, and their capacity to defend their political organization, the *capitanía*. This organization is not a "traditional" institution; rather, it is the result of relations with colonial powers and national society and of transformations within Guaraní society itself. Under political pressures, the threat of the loss of their territory, and hostile relations with white settlers, the Guaraní developed a centralized institution and maintained collective loyalties. The *capitanía* is an organization formed by supracommunal chiefs (of a number of linked communities), communal chiefs, elders, advisors, and mayors. This organization has been influenced and transformed by factors such as the entry of *hacendados* (non-indigenous land owners) into the Izozo region, the Chaco War between Bolivia and Paraguay (1932–35), migrations to Argentina, and interaction with government authorities, anthropologists, and development agencies.

The Izoceño-Guaraní belong to the Tupí-Guaraní linguistic family. They are known in the ethnographic literature as Chiriguanos, Izoceño-Guaraní, or Tapui. There are several other groups in the same linguistic family in Bolivia (Sirionó, Yuqui, Guarayos), but only two others, the Ava and the

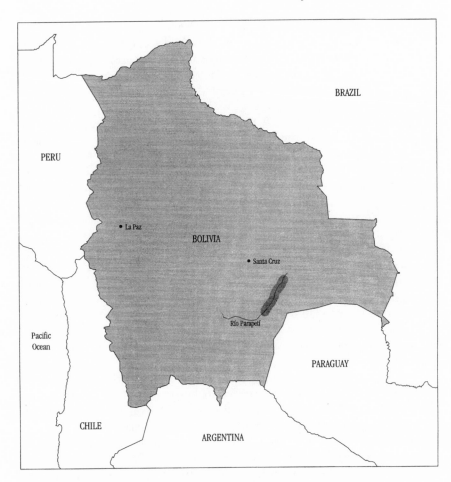

Map 4. Izoceño Communities along the Parapetí River

Simba, share common cultural and linguistic elements with the Izoceños. I use the terms Izoceño and Guaraní because these are used by the group itself. The term Izoceño refers to their geographical location in the Izozo region. The term Guaraní, by contrast, encompasses numerous indigenous groups from Brazil and Paraguay to Bolivia and Argentina and has become a term that represents political and cultural vindication and the emergence of a pan-Guaraní identity.

The Izoceños are a mestizo people, a blend of Chané (Arawak linguistic family) and Guaraní Indians who migrated to Bolivia during the fourteenth and fifteenth centuries. The fusion of these two groups gave rise to what is known in the historical sources as Chiriguano Indians. The Chiriguano enslaved and subjected to cannibalism the less bellicose Chané. The present-day Izoceños are the result of this process of *mestizaje*, with the addition of

Chiriguano Indians who were escaping the wars against the Spanish during the sixteenth century. This group adapted to the dry and hostile environment of the Izozo region and maintained many common features (language, economy, religious practices, and so on) with groups of the eastern slopes of the Andes (Ava and Simba). The total population in the Izozo region is approximately 9,000 individuals.

The Izoceño-Guaraní identify themselves as authentic Guaraní and differentiate themselves from the Chané slaves and the Ava of the cordillera region. The Izoceños live in the Izozo (province of Cordillera, department of Santa Cruz, Bolivia), which in Guaraní means "water that is cut off" (*agua cortada*). This refers to the irregular course of the Parapetí River, which during the dry season dries up completely. The Izoceños are settled in sixteen communities bordering the Parapetí River and are sedentary agriculturists who also practice fishing and hunting. Although they were evangelized by Franciscan missions during the nineteenth century, permanent missions were not established in the region. In the 1920s Anglican missions were established in the area known as Bajo Izozo. Currently, half of the communities belong to evangelical churches. During the nineteenth century, white ranchers settled in Izoceño lands and usurped part of their territory, forcing them to work in their haciendas. Every year, a significant part of the population engages in seasonal migration to the sugarcane plantations, timber mills, and cotton harvest of Bolivia.

The ethnographic and ethnohistorical literature on the Chiriguano is abundant. Franciscan missionaries contributed important ethnographies (Niño 1912, 1918), grammars, and dictionaries (Giannecchini 1916). Ethnohistorical studies of this group are significant, and many focus on origins (Susnik 1968, 1975; Saignes and Combès 1994), missionaries (Langer 1987; Saignes 1984, 1985b), and warfare (Saignes 1974, 1985a). The writings of ethnographers Erland Nordenskiöld and Alfred Métraux are indispensable references for the study of the Chiriguano (Nordenskiöld 1912, 1920; Métraux 1930, 1931a, 1931b, 1948). Contemporary ethnographic studies have focused on religion (Riester et al. 1979; Riester 1984, 1986), oral tradition (Simon de Souza 1987), and political organization (Hirsch 1991). Publications on the Ava-Guaraní are more prolific than on the Izoceños, although many of the recent ethnographies and ethnohistorical studies include data on the Izoceños (Pifarre 1986, 1989; Albó 1990; Meliá 1988). In the last few years, numerous anthropologists and sociologists have visited Guaraní communities; the results of their studies are yet to be seen, but will surely contribute to a more complex understanding of these communities.

This chapter explores how Guaraní political leaders and their political practices and organizations serve to empower a disenfranchised group. The chief's fundamental role has been that of peacemaker and orator. His leadership is based on hereditary succession and cannot exert coercive authority. Since the decision-making process depends on consensus achieved at communal and supracommunal assemblies, the chief acts as an executor of the society's decisions. Although these characteristics constitute a continuity from the past, there are also new demands placed on the *mburuvisa* (chief). As a result of relations with the national society and the needs and expectations that arose therefrom, the *mburuvisa* became a cultural broker and began to concentrate his efforts on getting resources for his people. The *mburuvisa* developed strategies as well as networks and relations with governmental and nongovernmental organizations (NGOs) in order to secure these objectives. The *capitanía* has achieved many of its goals and has fostered the development of a pan-Indian organization in eastern Bolivia. The emergence of the *capitanía* in the national political arena has allowed the Guaraní, together with the highlands peoples (Aymara and Quechua), to be part of a national debate on pluriculturalism and of a process of political participation involving indigenous peoples in Bolivia.

The main focus of this chapter is to understand how the Guaraní strengthened their political organization, used it to struggle for the group's interests and needs, and developed new political practices. These practices include redefining relations with white ranchers, establishing contact with NGOs, and strengthening the role of the *capitanía*. The chapter has three parts. The first presents a description of the main components of the *capitanía* and the way in which these components articulate their activities. The second part deals with the historical factors that led to the process of institutional building and collective action. The third examines the emergence of pan-Indian organizations and their link to NGOs and the state. We consider the Guaraní to be active political actors engaged in their own decision-making process and, although living in a situation of socioeconomic marginality, actively participating in the country's public and political spheres.

ETHNOGRAPHIC SETTING

When I began my fieldwork, I chose to stay in a community known as La Brecha, originally named Guirayoasa (where birds fly by), because it is the headquarters of the *capitanía*. This is the village where the *capitán* lives and where most important meetings are held. Overall, communities range in size from ten to seventy houses, inhabited by groups of extended families. The communities are not settled in a fixed pattern, although some have a central plaza area used as a soccer field, near to which there is a water pump, a school, an evangelical church, a health post, and a consumer cooperative.

A household consists of a house (one or two rooms), a granary to store corn, squash, beans, and other crops, and a kitchen area. Some households lodge a nuclear family, but in most cases an extended family dwells in a household. The members of an extended family (with predominant, although not exclusive, matrilocal residence) build their houses next to each other. Thus a family group of twenty people may live in three or four different houses, but share the kitchen area. A few families have a corral near their house where they keep calves and milking cows. The houses are built of adobe bricks or branches filled with mud, and the roofs are either thatched or made of discarded cane stalks or corrugated zinc. In some communities, tiles are made for the roofs.

The Chaco region has a large variety of trees and plants providing fruits and vegetables. Fruits such as *algarroba* (*Prosopis juliflora*) are ground and the resulting flour fermented into a beverage. Other fruits such as *mistol* (*Zyzyphus mistol*) and *chañar* (*Geoffroae decorticans*) are also collected. The *caraguatá* (*Bromelia serra*) is a plant of many uses: the fibrous leaves are used to make ropes, the stem is roasted and eaten, and the fruit is boiled to obtain a thick syrup. Children participate actively in the gathering of wild fruits.

Most Guaraní families raise domestic animals such as cows, pigs, goats, and sheep. Livestock animals are either butchered for local consumption or used for sale to or barter with merchants in order to purchase consumer items such as sugar, *mate*, flour, soap, clothes, oils, and batteries. The animals roam freely around the village and frequently break into the fields and eat up the crops. Since colonial times when cattle were introduced, and since the establishment of haciendas, the Izoceños have raised livestock for income and food. Low agricultural yield, lack of access to markets, and ecological deterioration have led to a significant out-migration in search of work, further decreasing the agricultural production. Many Guaraní receive salaries by working as teachers or hospital personnel or for NGOs. Charagua, the nearest train station and town, is 100 kilometers away from the central community of La Brecha, and it links the town of Yacuiba, bordering on Argentina in the south, to the city of Santa Cruz to the north. The other means of access to the Izozo is by road to Santa Cruz, which is 350 kilometers to the northwest. Although during part of the year the roads are impassable due to the rains, most of the year the Izozo is a very dry and windy region. Several communities have changed their location as a result of the changing course of the river and ecological factors, such as droughts and floods. According to a 1920 census, there were twenty-five to twenty-seven communities in the Izozo. In a map of Bolivia dated 1945, the majority of the communities were located on the eastern margin of the river, known as La Banda. Currently there are five communities on the eastern margin of the Parapetí River (Pifarre 1986:34). Lack of access to water, together with ecological erosion and inadequate roads, has been a major obstacle to development in the Izozo.

THE *CAPITANÍA* OF THE IZOZO: THE EMERGENCE OF A NATIVE POLITICAL ORGANIZATION

During the 1980s in Bolivia, the *capitanía* became a model of native political organization based on indigenous political practices. This organization symbolized a step toward the self-determination of indigenous peoples.

The *capitanía* influenced the reorganization and emergence of *capitanías* among other Guaraní groups in Bolivia and is recognized at the national level as a legitimate political body. The Izoceños take pride in their *capitanía*; they acknowledge that through this organization they have secured land titles and obtained assistance from NGOs and the government.

The term *capitanía* derives from the word *capitán* (captain) in reference to Spanish military rank. The term *capitán* is found in the chroniclers of the seventeenth century and is used among other native groups in South America to refer to their chiefs. Nowadays, the Izoceños use the term *mburuvisa* (leader) and *capitán* alternately.

At the supracommunal level, the most important authority is the *mburuvisa guasu* (*capitán grande* in Spanish). The primary distinguishing feature of this leader is his position based on hereditary succession. The *mburuvisa guasu* acts as a peacemaker or mediator, a cultural broker, mediating between Izoceños and the national society. Each individual village has a *capitán* or *mburuvisa*. These are the representatives of the people at the local level who speak for the community at the level of the *capitanía*. Although it is not a prerequisite for a village *mburuvisa* to belong to a family of leaders, throughout the Izozo there are "lineages" of leaders who are decisively involved in political and economic matters. Those who belong to a family of leaders can be found holding important positions in development projects implemented by NGOs and in the evangelical church.

"It's in the Blood": Inheriting the Office

When Boni Chico, as the youngest son of Bonifacio Barrientos Iyambae, inherited the position of *mburuvisa guasu* from his father in his late twenties, he was inexperienced and thought that under no circumstance could he take on such a formidable task. At first he declined and did not accept this nomination, but the elders and leaders persuaded him to accept this role; they insisted that they would guide and support him. I wondered why the people had backed him, why the Izoceños submitted to the leadership of a man who did not want to be a chief and who appeared to lack the skills required for such a role. I would find the answers to these questions during my fieldwork.

One of the most persistent elements of the *capitanía* is that the position of *mburuvisa guasu*, the highest rank in the leadership structure, is inherited. It is a position passed down from father to son; when the father is too old or dies, his son becomes *mburuvisa guasu*. Regardless of age, the son must accept his new position. Occasionally, there have been modifications to this pattern and a nephew, cousin, or brother has been appointed.

The position of *mburuvisa guasu* always remains within the ruling family. This family bears the surname Iyambae (without owner). Although some descendants of the Iyambae family also have the last name Barrientos, they are all proud of their ancestral last name Iyambae. They refer to themselves as those who cannot be dominated, who are free and independent. The Iyambae and their descendants are a family with great prestige and high status.

The *mburuvisa guasu* must acquire three fundamental skills: (*a*) oratorical ability, (*b*) skills as a peacemaker, and (*c*) courageousness. Being a leader includes certain privileges, such as communal labor in his fields, exemption from participating in communal work, and differential and privileged treatment.

"A good *mburuvisa* is one who knows how to speak well to the people" is a remark often heard among the Guaraní when they mention the main characteristics of a *mburuvisa*. According to Lowie (1967:76): "A third tribute of civil leadership is the gift of oratory, normally to be exercised on behalf of tribal harmony and good old traditional ways. . . . a Chiriguano explained to Nordenskiöld the existence of a female head of the tribe: her father had taught her to speak in public."

A chief must be able to speak with eloquence, but must not express himself in an aggressive manner nor insist on his point of view. Instead, he must carefully and calmly present his ideas. When conflict arises in a community, the chief must dwell on the importance of living in peace, cooperating with the communal authorities, and collaborating for the village's progress. The *mburuvisa*'s speech is repetitive. However, when there is a major assembly of the *capitanía* in which new projects are proposed, his speech becomes innovative. It is most common for the *mburuvisa guasu* to deliver a speech that manifests his role as peacemaker. The *mburuvisa* must never express a direct accusation against an individual who has been charged with theft or witchcraft. Instead, he must eloquently avoid aggressive behavior. His fundamental task is to mediate at the assembly by appeasing the village and soothing grievances.

This gift of oratory is transmitted from generation to generation and is also the specific domain of the *ñee iya* (owners of the word). As peacemaker or mediator, the *mburuvisa* must be able to achieve consensus at the communal and supracommunal levels. In so doing, he cannot impose his opinions or his will on the people and must be ready to accept the decisions of the group. Boni Chico is constantly invited to attend meetings regarding dispute resolution. Conflicts arise involving witchcraft accusations, theft, tensions with neighboring ranchers, divorce, and adultery. Boni patiently listens to all the parties, and when it is his time to talk, his words are neutral but firm. If no consensus is reached, Boni will dictate a sentence. Boni's even-tempered character is one of his main strengths; he avoids isolating anyone, and when difficulties arise, he relies on his advisors for counsel and support.

The *Mburuvisa* as Broker

The consolidation and growth of the political organization are the result of the chiefs' struggles to obtain land titles and government recognition of their leadership. At the turn of the century, the chiefs became the representatives of the people and began to establish contact with governmental authorities. In order to obtain resources, the chiefs needed to become mediators between the communities, the *hacendados*, the missionaries, and government representatives. The role of the *mburuvisa* as broker began to change at the end of the nineteenth century, in particular when the Izoceños, together with other indigenous peoples of the highlands, were hired to work at the sugarcane plantations established in northern Argentina. In some cases, chiefs who spoke and read Spanish were hired by owners of sugarcane plantations as labor recruiters. This led to a change in the role of the *mburuvisa*, who now wielded economic power, negotiated with the bosses, and exercised power over his people (Bernand 1973).

During the 1950s, the chiefs once more became labor recruiters at the newly established sugarcane plantations of Santa Cruz in northern Bolivia. This role led to a loss of prestige and abusive behavior by some *mburuvisas* who acquired economic and political power, which led many of them to mismanage the salaries of workers. Such chiefs are criticized by the Izoceños; they exemplify the ambiguous situation in which they are caught when dealing with the national society. Co-optation, either economic or political, has been a constant threat for the *capitanía*.

The late *mburuvisa guasu*, Bonifacio Barrientos Iyambae, was a chief for almost half a century and carried out major transformations in the *capitanía*. He was concerned with improving the socioeconomic situation of his people and thought that the only way this could be achieved was by strengthening and transforming the *capitanía* and its political strategies. A more "modern" and efficient approach to leadership emerged, built upon a new discourse centered on development and progress. The leaders became resource brokers who must contact government agencies, NGOs, church groups, and others as a means of achieving support and funding for development projects.

Decentralizing Power: The Support System of the *Capitanía*

One of the first leaders I met in the Izozo to attract my attention was Dario Ñandureza. He was in his fifties, quite outspoken, energetic, and at times explosive. He presented himself as the *segundo capitán* (the second captain) and told me that he had been a chief since the late *Capitán Grande* Bonifacio Barrientos appointed him in 1967. Ñandureza learned from the advice of Barrientos and from accompanying him to assemblies and on travels. A native of the community of Copere in the Alto Izozo, Ñandureza worked for many years as a labor contractor until he became a chief. The position of *segundo capitán* is ranked second in the hierarchy after the *mburuvisa guasu* and includes a jurisdiction of three communities from Copere to Yapiroa, which is the most populated area of the Izozo. His duties include attending meetings and traveling throughout the Izozo and to the city. He must act as a representative of the *mburuvisa guasu* and of the *capitanía* to governmental authorities or institutions.

The *segundo capitán* has become very skillful in dealing with the bureaucracy; he travels frequently to La Paz to visit the different ministries and work on obtaining land titles and other matters. Throughout the years the *segundo capitán* has become a staunch supporter of the *capitanía* and will defend the *mburuvisa guasu* against any attack. On more than one occasion, I have witnessed the way Ñandureza not only defended the *capitanía*'s authority but also made a point of not allowing intromission from outside authorities into internal matters. By creating this position, the *mburuvisa guasu* was delegating responsibilities, decentralizing his power, and at the same time forming stronger alliances within the region. In Guaraní society, the *mburuvisa guasu* should not concentrate power, because this would go against Guaraní notions of consensual decision making and individual autonomy much cherished among them.

Elders as Cultural Reservoir: The *Arakua Iya* (Owners of Knowledge) and *Ñee Iya* (Owners of the Word)

Among the Guaraní, elders are not marginalized from society, but are highly respected. When I began doing fieldwork in the Izozo, people would suggest that I talk to the elderly; they would give me specific names and tell me that those persons really knew about the old days; they knew "our history." I spent many hours visiting and recording interviews with elders. Elders constitute the depositories of cultural heritage and are in charge of keeping alive the history and values of the Izoceños. Political innovation and modernization have not impaired the status of the elders. Furthermore, elders help the younger generation by providing counseling and support and allowing the latter to participate as long as they are committed to the groups' values. Although there have been a few cases in which the elders have tried to form factions against the *mburuvisa guasu*, they will promote unity in spite of personal differences.

Elders can occupy two very important positions within the *capitanía* as *arakua iya* (counselors) and as *ñee iya* (orators). The *arakua iya* (*arakua*: knowledge, wisdom, advice; *iya*: owner) are wise men who are knowledgeable about the history and myths, and their function is to counsel the chiefs. Although they tend to preserve the "traditional" Izoceño ways, they are open to innovations and support the ideas of the younger generation. The *arakua iya* are not as visible as other members of the *capitanía*, and their participation in assemblies is not required, but they do provide advice both in times of crisis and in everyday events.

The *ñee iya* (*ñee*: work; *iya*: owner) are the society's orators who give long speeches that reinforce "traditional" values, myths, and history. They master the art of oratory in long and elaborate speeches referring to past experience and historical events that can serve as guides to solve present-day problems. The *ñee iya* have a tendency to exaggerate and to give repetitive speeches that serve as lessons in history for the younger generation. They intervene actively when conflicts arise and deliver speeches to pacify situations. Together with the *arakua iya*, the *ñee iya* provide important support for the *capitanía*. By intervening in moments of crisis with their speeches and counseling, these elders help defuse tensions and work toward achieving consensus.

Traditionally the *mburuvisa guasu* was advised by the *arakua iya*, but ever since he began to travel frequently and establish contact with governmental authorities and NGOs, he has depended on a new type of advisor to assist him and represent him during his absence. These advisors, known as *asesores*, are a recent innovation. They are not elders, but belong to a younger generation that has more experience with the national society; they are bilingual and know how to negotiate with outsiders. These advisors are informed of what is happening in the communities and of the development projects that are being implemented in the region. They do not make decisions, but express their opinions to the *mburuvisa guasu*.

The advisors constitute the consultative body of the *capitanía*. They act at two levels: (1) the community and (2) the *capitanía*. The current *mburuvisa guasu* has two advisors whom he has chosen and who live in his same village, and a body of advisors who have been elected in each village of the Izozo. But in order to establish a flow of communication between the leaders and the villagers, the *capitanía* must rely on the *iwira iya* (mayors). These men are in charge of informing every household about the time and place of meetings, the communal labor, or festivities, and they must ensure that people attend. Thus, for the *capitanía* to be able to operate, all the components must interact with each other and reach the people. The only way to ensure this is to resort to the assembly.

The Backbone of the *Capitanía*: The Assembly

The *asamblea*, or assembly (*yemboati*, "to make union, to gather"), is the deliberative, judicial, and executive institution of the Izoceños. The assembly is the most pervasive element of Guaraní society. All community matters, including the supernatural, are dealt with in the assembly. In fact, its authority rests above the authority of the *mburuvisa guasu*. Given that among the Guaraní the chief cannot exert any type of coercive power, the *mburuvisa* must ultimately act in accordance with the decisions made by the assembly. There are two kinds of assemblies: the assembly of the *capitanía* and the communal assembly. The assembly of the *capitanía* is composed of the chiefs and representatives of all the communities of the Izozo and is convoked to discuss matters that affect all Izoceños.

The communal assembly is formed by all the members of a community who wish to attend and is convoked to discuss local matters. The assemblies (communal and supracommunal) are divided into two types: (*a*) specific assemblies to discuss development projects, land claims, and major meetings and (*b*) assemblies that deal with supernatural problems such as witchcraft accusations, droughts, or plagues caused by sorcerers. Assemblies organized to discuss problems regarding the supernatural are attended by the shamans. Some of these meetings have received NGO support, but they are generally organized and supported by the villages.

Decision-making power rests in the social body at large. Therefore, the *mburuvisa guasu*, or local chief, cannot make nor implement any decision by himself; he is subject to the authority of the assembly of *capitanes*. The chiefs cannot impose their will over the people at the assembly. Individual autonomy is highly valued among the Izoceños; everybody has the right and liberty to express an opinion. However, if an individual does not agree with the decision made by the majority, the matter is discussed until group consensus is achieved. During my fieldwork, I attended many assemblies and was always struck by the orderly way in which they were conducted. Even in times of crisis and serious internal grievances, everyone was given an opportunity to voice an opinion. When the discussion became heated and there was strong disagreement, the *ñee iya* or *capitán* would intervene to appease disputing members. Decisions are always reached by achieving consensus. One of the worst criticisms that an Izoceño can raise against a chief is that he made a decision without consulting the assembly.

Historical Background and Collective Action

The Iyambae and Barrientos family of chiefs traces descent from José Iyambae and refers to him as *ñande ramui* (our grandfather). There are no exact dates indicating when he lived, although the Franciscan priest Lorenzo Calzavarini (1980:245) quotes a dialogue between the Franciscan priest Doroteo Giannecchini and the *mburuvisa* "Yambae" of the Izozo that took place between 1886 and 1887. Natalio Barrientos, a descendant of José Iyambae, mentioned to me that the son of José Iyambae, who became *mburuvisa guasu*, did not have government credentials. This allowed the white settlers to exploit and mistreat the Indians, because the latter could not defend themselves without official support. This would soon change, and the *mburuvisa guasu* would search for official government recognition.

The elders link the emergence of the *capitanía* as a stable institution to the entry of white settlers (*hacendados*) to the Izozo region. The first sustained contact with white settlers began in the 1860s. At that time there were political problems in Bolivia. In 1864 General Mariano Melgarejo, a military man, became president of Bolivia. His administration was authoritarian, and he eliminated his political adversaries. Many politicians were persecuted and sought refuge in the Indian territories. The elders remember that the first white man to enter the Izozo and to establish a hacienda (estate) was José Mercado, who marked the beginning of the usurpation of their territory.

After Mercado's death, the haciendas were subdivided and sold among his descendants and new owners. This allowed the entrance of more *hacendados* into the region. At this point, not only were the Izoceños deprived of their land, they were also subjected to ill-treatment and exploitation when they worked for the new landowners.

In the 1920s an episode took place that became a turning point in the relations between the Izoceños, settlers, and government authorities. Emilio Castro, a white rancher, wanted to force a man called Mikerante to work in his hacienda. Mikerante did not want to go, so he was threatened with severe punishment. He was ready to flee to Argentina when his relative, Enrique Iyambae, son of the late chief José Iyambae, was informed of this and decided to intervene. Iyambae told Mikerante not to leave. He borrowed his mule to go to meet with the government authorities and request them to put an end to the abuses to which they were subjected.

Enrique Iyambae visited a Protestant missionary in the town of San Francisco de Parapetí. The missionary wrote a letter for Enrique to present to the authorities in the town of Lagunillas, explaining the situation. When Enrique arrived at Lagunillas, he was asked who the *capitán* was, but the names he mentioned were not among those registered as *mburuvisa guasu*. The *subprefecto* (governmental authority) of Lagunillas gave Iyambae a note to take to the *corregidor* of the Izozo.[2] However, once he had arrived in Izozo and had sent the letter to the *corregidor*, he was put in the pillory as a punishment for leaving his village. Any villager required permission from the *corregidor* in order to leave his community.

In spite of all this, Enrique Iyambae continued with his protest. He went again to Lagunillas and was told by the *subprefecto* that they would meet in five days in the city of Santa Cruz. There they would corroborate whether the current *mburuvisa guasu*, named Kansu, was registered as chief. Enrique and the *subprefecto* of Lagunillas met in Santa Cruz and went to see the *prefecto* (governor). There they verified that the current chiefs, Kansu and Tamendasui, had not been registered. The *prefecto* then decided to name Enrique Iyambae as *mburuvisa guasu* of the Izozo.

The remarkable aspect of this episode was the intervention of national authorities in naming the chief and in creating a geopolitical division in the Izozo. The *prefecto* decided that, given the extention of the Izozo (at that time there were thirty-five communities), the region should be divided into two sections, the Bajo Izozo and the Alto Izozo, and thus two *mburuvisa guasu* should rule. Nobody wanted to accept the responsibility of being chief for fear of the white people, but Enrique Iyambae, who had lived in Argentina for many years and had learned to read, write, and speak Spanish fluently, agreed to be named *mburuvisa guasu* of the Bajo Izozo. His nephew Casiano Barrientos agreed to be the chief of the Alto Izozo.

The Izoceños accepted these two chiefs because they belonged to a family of leaders. This division led to factionalism between Alto Izozo and Bajo Izozo that has continued up to the present day. The intervention of governmental authorities in naming a *mburuvisa guasu* gave these leaders legitimacy at the regional and national levels by granting them official credentials. However, this did not imply that the government would end the abuses committed on the Indians or the appropriation of their territory. Nevertheless, it was the beginning of a long struggle. The official recognition of native leaders and their capacity to pursue collective goals by their own means constitutes a turning point in the process of institutional building of the *capitanía*. Since that time, the Guaraní have established active political relations with the outside world.

In 1927, under the government of Hernando Siles, a major event occurred in Izoceño history: Casiano Barrientos, his half brother Bonifacio Barrientos Iyambae, and seventeen other Guaraní walked all the way to La Paz to claim land titles and official recognition. This was the first of a series of epic trips to La Paz conducted by the Izoceños and their chiefs to defend their territory and their rights. The men suffered many hardships on this trip; some became ill, and several died. Although the government did not place much importance on the Guaraní, they nevertheless made a statement by going to La Paz and demonstrating that they were there to defend their rights.

In 1928 the Paraguayan army led an attack on a Bolivian fort. A few years later, in 1932, amid land claims and conflict with white settlers in the Izozo, the Chaco War broke out. The Izoceños found themselves torn between the two nations of Bolivia and Paraguay. Paradoxically, the Izoceños at that time knew more about northern Argentina than about Bolivia. The Guaraní were unaware at that time that the war was due to a conflict of oil interests in the Chaco created by Standard Oil Company. The Bolivian government gave the concession to the Standard Oil Company to exploit the oil in the Chaco region while that territory was in dispute between Bolivia and Paraguay.

By 1936 three years of a devastating war were over. Thousands of Izoceños had been taken as prisoners to Paraguay, many had died, and others had joined the Bolivian army, while others had fled to Argentina. Upon returning to the Izozo, they found their villages empty, their animals dispersed, and their crops gone. The people were uneasy about returning to the Izozo for fear of reprisal. The *mburuvisa guasu*, Casiano Barrientos, was executed in 1936 by a man called Julio Ortiz, a *hacendado* for whom the Indians worked. Enrique Iyambae had been living in Argentina and returned several years later.

The Izoceños were persecuted by governmental authorities. They were accused of treason because they had been prisoners of the Paraguayan army. To the Bolivian government, the Guaraní appeared as traitors who had helped the Paraguayan army find its way in the dry and desertlike Chaco. It was many years after the war, when schools were installed in the Izozo, men were drafted for military service, and labor migration toward Santa Cruz intensified, that a sense of Bolivian "national identity" would develop.

Bonifacio Barrientos Iyambae: The Emergence of a Leader

There was a void of leadership after the war, and Bonifacio Barrientos Iyambae, nephew of Enrique Iyambae, was requested by his people to return to the Izozo. Bonifacio had been a zapper for the Bolivian army and was living in hiding, fearing reprisals. He was persecuted also by the white settlers for his continued struggle for land titles. In 1942 his uncle Enrique Iyambae returned to the Izozo. Enrique settled in the community of Iyobi as *mburuvisa guasu* of the Bajo Izozo. During the presidency of Gualberto Villaroel, Bonifacio, his uncle Enrique, and his cousin Casia Iyambae traveled to La Paz. On this trip, both Bonifacio and Enrique obtained credentials as *mburuvisa guasu*. Bonifacio's jurisdiction was the same one that his half brother Casiano had once been appointed to, the Alto Izozo from Tamachindi to Copere. Enrique Iyambae continued to rule the Bajo Izozo from Coropo to Cuarirenda.

Bonifacio Barrientos had lived many years in Argentina, where he had worked at the sugarcane plantations of San Martín and Ledesma. As a result of this experience and his frequent trips throughout Bolivia, Barrientos began to develop ideas that would transform the political and social life of the Izozo. Among the Guaraní migrants, Argentina became known as *Mbaporenda*, the land where there is work. During their stays in Argentina, many learned Spanish, received some schooling, and were introduced to a different country, one in which they saw more progress. Barrientos and other leaders thought that this progress could be achieved by obtaining land titles, going to school, forming cooperatives, building a hospital, and fixing the roads (Hirsch 1991). His discourse was based on the idea of work for progress; this meant obtaining land titles and improving the standard of living by introducing cooperatives and development projects.

Moreover, Barrientos thought that a hostile confrontation with white settlers would not be productive for his people. Whites outnumbered them and were more powerful. The Izoceños were in need of allies and support in order to obtain titles and benefits from the government. If, for instance, the *mburuvisa* was in need of money to travel, he could count on the help of a neighboring *hacendado*. This politics of friendship with the *karai* (whites) does not necessarily lead to co-optation; neither does it imply that the Guaraní readily accept and trust the *karai* unconditionally, but it may lead to a more nuanced perception of non-Indians. The Izoceños were prioritizing the ends in spite of the means.

In the past, the chief's role had appeared only under special circumstances. In other words, the chiefs had exercised their role only in cases of warfare or when meetings were held because of witchcraft accusations. Bonifacio Barrientos changed the character of the chief's role by changing the character of the assembly. In these meetings, myths and history had been narrated or witchcraft accusations and marital problems had been ventilated. When Bonifacio Barrientos became a *mburuvisa guasu*, the assemblies were transformed into arenas in which plans and projects were discussed. At the assemblies, the chiefs gathered and discussed new ideas or projects to be implemented in the Izozo. The chiefs presented reports on their communities and the projects discussed at the communal assembly.

Bonifacio Barrientos also innovated the hierarchical structure of the *capitanía* system. He introduced chiefs for each community, because it was too difficult for him to attend to the problems of all the communities. As already mentioned, he introduced the role of the *segundo capitán* for the jurisdiction of three communities that include Copere, Capeatindi, and Yapiroa. In this way, he decentralized power and gave more autonomy to the communities while maintaining his contacts and his sources of information throughout the Izozo.

Changes in the *capitanía* or better relations with the *karai* did not suffice to achieve development and progress. Direct support in the forms of funding, education, and technical assistance was required to carry out projects. Although Bonifacio Barrientos was the main moving force, he was not alone in his plans and projects. He was backed up by the elders, the chiefs, and other collaborators.

NGOs and Pan-Indian Organization

The state's neglect of the economic and social needs of the indigenous peoples fostered the introduction of nongovernmental organizations in Bolivia (Bebbington and Thiele 1993). Development agencies have been allowed to implement projects without much interference from the state, thus leaving an arena for fostering political and social awareness, the training of native leaders, and the emergence of alternative political organizations. NGOs have been working among the Izoceños for the past twenty years. These are of a wide spectrum, ranging from church organizations (both Catholic and Protestant) to agencies directed by anthropologists or humanitarians. Thus their developmental objectives are different, and so has been their impact on native peoples. Many projects implemented by these agencies have gone beyond economic development and have aimed at fostering ethnic revival and developing new political organizations leading to self-determination. Native leaders found in these NGOs a vehicle to achieve their own political projects of land titles, self-determination, and a resource that would economically revitalize the communities and train leaders to deal more effectively with state institutions. With the help of NGO personnel, Izoceño leaders could now present specific demands, such as land titles, protection from outside encroachment, and improvement of their socioeconomic situation, in a more articulate fashion.

Two NGOs, one called Ayuda para el Campesino Indígena del Oriente Boliviano (APCOB) and the other Centro de Investigación y Promoción del Campesino (CIPCA), played a fundamental role in fostering the idea of economic development and sustainability and in leading to the emergence of two pan-Indian organizations. Although these NGOs are quite different in that APCOB was founded by anthropologists while CIPCA was established by the Jesuit order, both agencies emphasize self-determination and political participation by strengthening the role of the assembly and the *capitanía*. Development agencies have played a fundamental role in the Izozo by influencing the public discourse and political practices of the Guaraní. They have also created new expectations and needs. These changes, in turn, have led the Izoceños to respond to current transformations in a creative and flexible manner.

APCOB stimulated the emergence of the Central de Pueblos y Comunidades Indígenas del Oriente Boliviano (CIDOB), a pan-Indian organization that includes approximately eleven different indigenous groups of lowland Bolivia. CIPCA helped organize the Asamblea del Pueblo Guaraní (APG), an organization that unites Guaraní-speaking people. The NGOs' personnel have been instrumental in developing pan-Indian organization strategies at both political and economic levels and in making contacts with funding agencies and support groups at the international level. Without the support, both economic and political, of an NGO, it would have been very difficult and a lengthy process for an indigenous organization to develop. In contrast to the Bolivian highlands, where there is a longer history of political activism, in the eastern lowlands there were no antecedents of these types of political action.

In the case of CIDOB, its strength lies in the support it has received from organizations such as the *capitanía* and NGOs as well. Izoceño leaders are actively involved in the leadership structure of this organization and participate in meetings with government officials, including the president of Bolivia. In less than two decades, the confederation has become the most important and legitimate representative of the native peoples of eastern Bolivia.

When the Guaraní experienced encroachments into their territory and threats to their autonomy, the leadership developed strategies to confront these problems. The *mburuvisa* became a cultural broker, a leader skilled at negotiating with outsiders and capable of maintaining a delicate balance between the interests of the villagers and those of the white people. The *mburuvisa guasu* opted to befriend the outsiders. This did not imply acceptance of the outsiders' impositions, but constituted a viable strategy for obtaining resources for the communities. The *mburuvisa guasu* and the local chiefs are the representatives of the communities, but they cannot force or persuade the people to elect a specific person. Neither can they deliver orders or oblige the men to perform a task. Their leadership is based on consensus; they execute the decisions taken and agreed upon in the assemblies. The chief must promote solidarity and avoid conflict. He must be able to lead his people without threatening or imposing his demands or his opinion upon them. The role of the chief as one who "hunts and gathers" resources and deals with development and governmental agencies is an innovation that responds to specific needs and historical circumstances.

The transformations of the *capitanía* have been influenced by the incorporation of the indigenous political system within the boundaries of the nation-state. The central government has in turn accepted the *capitanía* as an administrative and representative institution. At the collective level, the Izoceños mobilized in a joint effort to support their chiefs as a means of achieving their goals.

The Guaraní face many challenges: permanent labor migration, ecological fragility of their environment, loss of their territory, pressures by political parties, evangelical sects, and internal factionalism. However, the *capitanía* is confronting these challenges, and if the economic achievements among the Guaraní have been modest, their political accomplishments have been concrete and long-lasting. The Guaraní have strengthened their organizational capacity and have taken control of development projects and decision making. The end result of this complex process has given the Guaraní a sense of empowerment.

POSTSCRIPT

In the last few years, Bolivia has undergone profound legislative changes that are having a sweeping impact upon native and peasant communities. In 1995 the Ley de Participación Popular was passed. This law decentralizes political power and reorganizes the role of the municipalities and the local communities. Communities are now organized as territorial base organizations (OTBs), the *capitanía* is considered one of these OTBs, and the Izozo region has become the first Indian municipality of Bolivia with its own mayor. This means that the Izozo will now receive funding from the government and have greater political autonomy. It also implies greater presence of political parties and the threat of co-optation of leaders to these parties. Another change has been educational reform and the implementation of bilingual and intercultural education. Izoceño children are being taught in Guaraní with new textbooks that reflect their sociocultural reality.

Finally, the Izoceños have obtained partial control of 2.5 million hectares of the newly constituted national park Gran Chaco. A group of Izoceños forms part of the board of directors. This, in turn, has brought heavy funding from international agencies for ecological and development projects in the Izozo region. The Izoceños through the *capitanía* are deciding who will implement projects, are forming part of NGO teams, and are involved in the decision-making process. The *capitanía* has its own office in the city of Santa Cruz, fully furnished with computers, secretaries, and a team of Izoceños and collaborators working on projects. As new challenges arise, the *capitanía* is at risk of losing touch with its bases and of not responding to the demands and needs of the people, but this is a risk that the leaders are aware of and are willing to confront.

NOTES

1. Research support for my fieldwork was provided by the Inter-American Foundation.
2. *Corregidor* is a representative of the national or departmental government. According to Pachón (1980:320), "The *corregidores* were the Spanish functionaries who were in charge of the administration and vigilance of the Indian villages. The *corregidor* and the priest were in charge of changing the indigenous political structure in order to adapt them to the colonial system."

REFERENCES

Albó, Xavier. 1990. *La comunidad hoy. Los Guaraní-Chiriguano*, vol. 3. La Paz: Centro de Investigación y Promoción del Campesino.

Bebbington, Anthony, and Graham Thiele. 1993. *Non-governmental Organizations and the State in Latin America*. London: Routledge.

Bernand, Carmen. 1973. La fin des capitaines. *Travaux de l'Institut Français d'Études Andines* 2(1):72–82.

Calzavarini, Lorenzo. 1980. *Nación Chiriguana: Grandeza y ocaso*. Bolivia: Amigos del Libro.

Giannecchini, Doroteo. 1916. *Diccionario Chiriguano-Español y Español-Chiriguano compilado teniendo a la vista diversos manuscritos de antiguos Misioneros del Apostólico Colegio de Santa María de los Ángeles de Tarija y particularmente el Diccionario Chiriguano Etimológico del R. P. Doroteo Giannecchini por los padres Santiago Romano y Herman Cattunar*. Tarija, Bolivia: a publication of the Franciscan Church.

Hirsch, Silvia. 1991. Political Organization among the Izoceño Indians of Bolivia. Ph.D diss., University of California at Los Angeles.

Langer, Erick. 1987. Franciscan Missions and Chiriguano Workers: Colonization, Acculturation, and Indian Labor in Southeastern Bolivia. *The Americas: A Quarterly Review of Interamerican Cultural History* 42(1):305–322.

Lowie, Robert. 1967. Some Aspects of Political Organization among the American Aborigines. In *Comparative Political Systems*, ed. Ronald Cohen and John Middleton, 63–87. Garden City: Natural History Press.

Meliá, Bartomeu 1988. *Ñande reko nuestro modo de ser y bibliografía general comentada*. Cuadernos de Investigación 30. La Paz: CIPCA.

Métraux, Alfred. 1930. Etudes sur la civilisation des Indiens Chiriguano. *Revista del Instituto de Etnología de la Universidad Nacional de Tucumán* 1:295–493.

————. 1931a. Les hommes-dieux chez les Chiriguanos et dans L'Amérique du Sud. *Revista del Instituto de Etnología de la Universidad Nacional de Tucumán* 2:61–91.

————. 1931b. Observaciones sobre la psicología de los Indios Chiriguano. *Solar* 1:89–122.

————. 1948. Tribes of the Eastern Slopes of the Bolivian Andes. In *Handbook of South American Indians*, ed. Julian Steward, 3:465–506. Washington, D.C.: Government Printing Office.

Niño, Fray Bernardino de. 1912. *Etnografía Chiriguana*. La Paz.

————. 1918. *Misiones Franciscanas del Colegio de Propaganda Fide de Potosi*. La Paz.

Nordenskiöld, Erland. 1912. *Indianerleben: El Gran Chaco* (Südamerika). Leipzig: Albert Bonnier.

————. 1920. *The Changes in the Material Culture of Two Indian Tribes under the Influence of New Surroundings*. New York: AMS Press.

Pachón, C., Ximena. 1980. Los Pueblos y los cabildos indígenas: La Hispanización de las culturas Americanas. *Revista Colombiana de Antropología* 23:297–326.

Pifarre, Francisco. 1986. Marco histórico de los Guaraníes de la Cordillera. In *Plan de Desarrollo Rural Cordillera Diagnóstico-Estrategia*. Vol. 2. Santa Cruz: Cordecruz-CIPCA.

————. 1989. *Chiríguano-Guaraní: Historia de un pueblo*. La Paz: CIPCA.

Riester, Jürgen. 1984. *Textos sagrados de los Guaraníes en Bolivia*. La Paz: Editorial Amigos del Libro.

————. 1986. Aspectos del chamanismo de los Izoceño-Guaraní. *Suplemento Antropológico* 21:263–283.

Riester, Jürgen, Barbara Riester, Barbara Schuchard, and Brigitte Simon. 1979. Los Chiriguano. *Suplemento Antropológico* 14(1–2):259–304.

Saignes, Thierry. 1974. Une frontiere fossile: La cordillière Chiriguano au XVIII siècle. Thèse de Doctorat, École Pratique des Hautes Études.

————. 1984. L'ethnographie missionnaire des Sauvages: La première description franciscaine des Chiriguano (1782). *Journal de la Société des Américanistes* 70:21–42.

————. 1985a. La guerra "salvaje" en los confines de los Andes y del Chaco: La resistencia Chiriguana a la colonización Europea. *Quinto Centenario* (Universidad Complutense de Madrid) 8:103–123.

————. 1985b. Sauvages et missionnaires: Les Sociétés de l'Oriente Bolivien à travers des sources missionaires récemment édité. *Caravelle: Cahiers du Monde Hispanique et Luso-Brésilien* 44:77–89.

Saignes, Thierry, and Isabelle Combès. 1994. Chiri-Guana: Nacimiento de una identidad mestiza. In *Chiriguano*, ed. Jurgen Riester, 25–201. Bolivia: APCOB.

Simon de Souza, Brigitte. 1987. *"Don Patron": Die Weissen in der oralen Tradition bolivianischer Indianer*. Studien und Dokumente zur Geschichte der romanischen Literaturen 19. Frankfurt, Germany: Peter Lang.

Susnik, Branislava. 1968. *Chiriguanos I: Dimensiones etnosociales*. Asunción, Paraguay: Museo Etnográfico "Andrés Barbero."

————. 1975. *Dispersión Tupí-Guaraní prehistórica*. Asunción, Paraguay: Museo Etnográfico "Andrés Barbero."

5

The Western Toba: Family Life and Subsistence of a Former Hunter-Gatherer Society

Marcela Mendoza

Previous anthropological studies on the family life of the Western Toba were completed before the 1950s, at a time when the bands were still foraging their land, and the people were less interested than today in participating in the life of the Bolivian, Paraguayan, and Argentinean nation-states. As a consequence, anthropologists and missionaries were fascinated by the most unexpected aspects of Toba livelihood, like the collective winter fishing, the head and scalp hunting, the practice of shamanism, and the mythology; but they overlooked many other, perhaps less impressive, aspects of the indigenous ways of living that were normal for people in those days.

In this chapter, I will discuss common characteristics of Toba livelihood overlooked in previous studies. Some of these aspects of everyday living are still meaningful for the people today. Others, like the extension of the former territories of the bands and the description of their seasonal foraging, are no longer in use. The Toba people have kept these memories about the recent past as part of an oral tradition that contributes to the definition of their contemporary sense of cultural identity.

Although my arguments build upon the background provided by previous studies, the discussion of this chapter relies primarily on my field data, which come from interviews and observations recorded during extended fieldwork among the Toba of western Formosa Province in Argentina.[1] Today the natural and social environments of the western Chaco differ enormously from what the anthropologists of the early 1900s had observed. Nevertheless, foraging activities still provide half of the daily subsistence for the families in some settlements. At certain times of the year, the contribution of fish, game, vegetables, and agricultural products to family diets increases up to 70 percent (Gordillo 1995:119). Other sources of income include wage labor, welfare, government subsidies, and the commoditization of agricultural products and crafts (see Peterson 1991).

The Toba people of western Formosa, who constitute a population of some 1,200 individuals, live on the right side of the Pilcomayo River in three main villages and several small settlements scattered over 35,000 hectares of their own land (De la Cruz and Mendoza 1989). There is also a Toba settlement in the town of Ingeniero Juárez, about eighty kilometers to the south. The Toba people reach out of their land for employment and education, just as government officials, merchants, and other agents reach into the communities to offer provisions and services. This dynamic process continuously opens up new opportunities for the people involved.

Instead of engaging in violent confrontations with whites, the Toba people now exercise other forms of "everyday resistance" to political and economic domination that are largely nonviolent, undertaken by individuals or small clusters of related families for their own particular reasons, and pursued without group strategy and organization. During the last eighty years, the Toba have managed to deactivate a "war complex" that was very active in the early 1900s. For this reason, the basic meaning of the outline that I describe in the second part of this study—the social control of internal aggression, gender differences in the expression of aggression, and how they reflect upon child socialization—contains very important elements to understand how Toba society actually works today.

THE WESTERN TOBA AND NEIGHBORING ETHNIC GROUPS

From the time they were first mentioned in colonial records, the Western Toba have populated both sides of the upper Pilcomayo River. By the 1700s priests and colonial administrators had written about the Toba people of the upper Pilcomayo River.[2] In the 1860s the Franciscan missionary Father José Cardús (1886:265) estimated their total number at about 4,000 individuals. In retrospect, Cardús's estimation appears to be fair, considering that in the same years, Campos (1888:246) estimated the number of indigenous people populating both sides of the Pilcomayo at less than 40,000.

The people we call Western Toba are not a unified ethnic group, but several independent groups that live in the western Chaco region (Miller 1979:53). They have been referred to as "Bolivian Toba" (Chervin 1908; Karsten 1923; Koch 1902; Shapiro 1962) and also as "Toba-Pilagá" (Métraux 1937; Nordenskiöld 1912). These different independent groups speak the same language and recognize the existence of social ties and cultural similarities between each other.

The Toba of Bolivia live today in the Province of Gran Chaco, Department of Tarija. Between 1860 and 1873 some of these bands settled in San Francisco Mission (Karsten 1932:30). They were later known as "Toba of

Villa Montes" by reference to the town located near the intersection of the Pilcomayo River and the 21°10′ parallel. In the late 1800s other Bolivian Toba lived near the intersection of the Pilcomayo and the 22° parallel (Nordenskiöld 1912). They were later known as "Toba of Monte Carmelo" by reference to the town located in Salta Province, Argentina (Tomasini 1976). Another Western Toba group used to have its territory on the upper Bermejo River (Cárlsen [1871], in Siegrist de Gentile 1982:214). Some of these Toba live today in the towns of Embarcación and Tartagal, Salta Province, Argentina. According to the Provincial Institute for Indigenous Communities, the Toba of Salta number about 800 individuals (De la Cruz 1989:97). Many of these Toba immigrated to the upper Bermejo from Villa Montes and the Pilcomayo River (Palavecino 1942:61). The Toba previously referred to as "Toba-Pilagá" live in western Formosa Province, Argentina, near the intersection of the Pilcomayo River and the Tropic of Capricorn.

Today, the most outspoken Western Toba individuals are proud to say that they are "pure Toba." This affirmation of authenticity sounds familiar to any reader of anthropology. However, in the case of the Western Toba, the statement proves to be historically true, as they were the members of the extended Guaycurúan linguistic family addressed as "Toba" by the neighboring Chiriguano. The Chaco region itself was located for the first time, in a map of the year 1650, in the land where the Western Toba lived—in the northwestern Chaco, between the 18° and 23° parallels (Tissera 1972:48).

The neighboring groups most frequently mentioned by the Toba peoples themselves, and who appear most often in the anthropological literature, are the Chiriguano, the Chorote, the Wichí, the Nivaclé, and the Pilagá (see Karsten 1932). With all of them, the Toba have made alliances, fought wars, and traded at different times under various circumstances. All indigenous groups of the western Chaco have related to each other in this ambivalent manner: they either raided each other's villages to take revenge for a previous attack, or they traded goods and invited each other to participate in games, dances, and drinking feasts. This alternation of periods of peace and times of war is characteristic of the history of Chaco groups at the end of the nineteenth century. It created the condition for the emergence of strong leaders, like Taycolique. Karsten (1923:6) interviewed Taycolique in 1912 while the Bolivian Toba were working at a sugarcane plantation in Salta Province, Argentina. Nordenskiöld (1912:9) wrote the following about him: "On the Argentine territory, the Toba chief *Taycolique* has systematically armed his warriors with rifles. He has cared about changing their equipment; instead of the old Remingtons, they now have more efficient repeating rifles."

In the late 1800s the territories of each ethnic group were separated by buffer zones. Every native or foreign traveler had to be well aware of the dangers of being caught in these no-man's-lands. In 1903, for example, the explorer Domingo Astrada (1906:124) reported that a group of Toba leaders and warriors asked him to join forces to attack together a neighboring

Nivaclé village. In 1909 the anthropologist Erland Nordenskiöld (1912:18) was asked by the Nivaclé to raid with them a Toba village. He declined to accept the offer, yet collected the scalp of a Toba warrior taken previously by the Nivaclé as a war trophy (Nordenskiöld 1919:184). Toba and Nivaclé warriors raided each other's territories until the early 1930s (Palavecino 1928:189; Rýden 1935). As recently as the 1990s, descriptions of the most appropriate technique to dry a human scalp were an interesting topic in my conversations with elder Toba.

The Toba not only fought against neighboring tribes, but also against whites. Even though the first white colonists arrived at the Bolivian borders of Toba land early in the 1600s, the criollos (whites of mixed European and Indian descent) did not thoroughly colonize the land on both margins of the river until the beginning of the 1900s. The Toba fought against the penetration of the criollos as much as they could. Bolivian and Argentine officials who participated in military expeditions to the upper Pilcomayo have recorded in vivid terms the battles of soldiers against coalitions of Toba warriors (Baldrich 1889; Campos 1888; Thouar 1891).

Toba active resistance to colonization has earned them the title of "ferocious warriors." In the early 1900s Koch (1902:3) wrote, "Even now, the words fire and murder are closely associated with the dreaded name 'Toba.' Despite the centuries-long efforts of the three states Argentina, Paraguay, and Bolivia, the Toba are the absolute masters of a vast territory." From 1915 to 1918, Western Toba bands participated in a movement intended to drive white people from Toba land. After taking many lives from both parties, this "rebellion" was suppressed by the Argentine army in cooperation with colonists. Since then, criollo cattle ranchers have fully occupied the land.

THE TOBA OF WESTERN FORMOSA PROVINCE, ARGENTINA

As long as their oral tradition can recall, the Toba of western Formosa Province have inhabited the land where they live today, on both margins of the Pilcomayo River. When the elders are asked about the extent of their former land, they say that it used to extend up to the dry beds of the river, now in Paraguay (Tebboth 1989:85). The Pilcomayo has changed its course more than once in historical times; two dry beds now lie in the Paraguayan Chaco, and another one lies south of its actual course in the Argentine Chaco (Cordini 1947:6). Toba mythology attributes the frequent movements of the riverbeds to the changing mood of a trickster (for an analysis of explanatory tales involving tricksters, see Ventur 1991).

In the early 1900s the Pilcomayo provided the axis for all areas trekked by Toba bands. Along this axis, the range of the areas trekked by the bands is shown in map 5. The upstream bands (the Uagadiacapi, the Quiliquipi, and

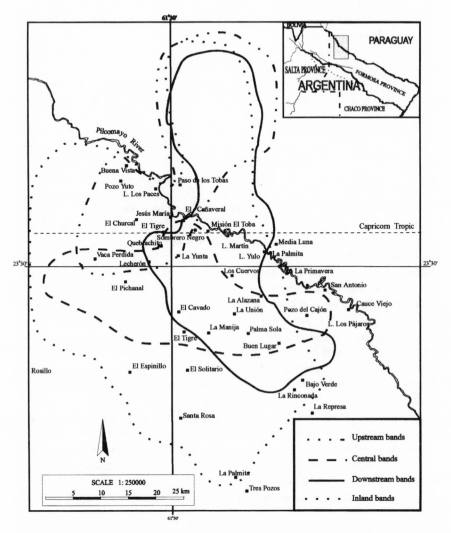

Map 5. Areas Trekked by the Toba of West Formosa, 1920s–1940s

the Nolagaic'pi) trekked mostly north of the river. The Nolagaic'pi people lived at the edge of the buffer zone that separated the Toba from the Wichí-Cagaicpi bands. The central bands were the ones that lived at the core of Toba land. Four different bands camped there (the Loliagadipi, the Quedo-copi, the Cotepi, and the Pejodipi). The downstream people were called Chiyagadipi. They used to trek the land north of the Pilcomayo, but they would also camp frequently to the south and southeast of Toba land. The Chiyagadipi lived at the border of a zone that separated the Toba from the

Pilagá and from the Nivaclé-Tiagaiquipi.[3] Bands living in the interior, both north and south of the river, were called Piogodipi, Maingodipi, and Jelcaicpi. They used to trek even further to the southwest, reaching the Toba group of the upper Bermejo River.

BAND MEMBERSHIP

Today, the composition of bands is not self-evident from the observation of people's behavior because the Toba do not move from place to place throughout the year anymore. Rather, they live in permanent villages (inhabited by individuals from several bands) and small settlements (inhabited by members of one or two bands). The social units I call bands are groups of extended families identified by others with a proper name. These extended families consider each other relatives. They used to live and trek together in the same area. Anthropologists described a similar organization in bands identified by proper names ("named bands") among many Chaco indigenous societies; for example, among the Eastern Toba, the Pilagá, the Wichí, the Nivaclé, and the Chamacoco.

Bands were flexible in both membership and size. A variety of residential arrangements were considered acceptable as individuals came together or broke apart into smaller groups. For example, in the 1910s the people called Maingodipi trekked the land, divided into at least three smaller groups of about thirty to forty members each. They would reunite from season to season and considered themselves close kin, as if they were actually trekking together all year round.

Most of the adults I have questioned about the subject answered that in the old times their parents used to live in camps of about five to seven huts (several individuals actually counted the huts and named about thirty-five persons by heart). However, in recent times, some Toba bands have chosen to live in larger villages. I calculate that in the old times the number of persons in each band fluctuated between thirty-five to seventy persons.

LEADERSHIP

By the 1900s the leader of a band was also a warrior-killer. He assumed the role of protector and defender of his relatives against other groups. Inside his band, the leader was a talker and an advisor. He would not make important decisions without the consensus of the elders and warriors.

Shamans also had an active political role as counselors and supporters of actions planned in cooperation among different bands. Each group of extended families had at least one shaman (a man or a woman) living with it. If the shaman of a group died, it had to find another person to perform this role (Métraux 1946b:17). Shamans and warriors were incorporated into the social network of a band by marriage.

EXTENDED FAMILIES

Missionary Dora Tebboth (1989:117) wrote in 1941: "Tobas live in family groups, grandparents, parents, uncles and aunts, brothers and children in clusters of huts." Each extended family could include parents, grandparents, children, spouses of married children, grandchildren, adopted children, and a widow or widower elder with no other family support, all of them living together in the same hut or in huts arranged in proximity. Each extended family had its own fire, and family members ate together. Members of the family ordinarily shared food.

The families "recruited" young and capable men by keeping an uxorilocal residence after marriage (the man came to live with his wife's family). They also sent their young men to marry women in other bands. This is how alliances were built. However, if the son of a leader proved to be a good and charismatic person like his father, he might be called back to lead the band at his father's death.

Band members passed their names from one generation to another by naming their children after great-grandparents or blood relatives who had died a generation before. The old people were in charge of finding an appropriate name for a newborn because they knew better the names of the folks of the previous generation. This custom served to maintain the idea of a stable band composition and the idea of membership persistence throughout time. It also provided a reference to identify band members who did not reside with the band. For example, someone old enough to know could identify the band membership of another individual just by listening to his or her name. Often during my interviews, a person would say, "Her name belongs to Uagadiacapi, and his belongs to Quiliquipi," because the person knew the ancestors of that individual.

KINSHIP

Band members considered each other kin and called each other, according to age and gender, "brother," "sister," "father," "son," "granddaughter," and so on. If someone wanted to refer, for example, to her or his biological sister, she or he should say "my *own* sister," emphasizing it with the proper term. After a time, individuals from different bands who had come to live in the same camp would be called brothers, sisters, grandsons, and so on, as if they were blood relatives. By this procedure, band members created social bonds. Kinship bonds and common residence presupposed economic cooperation and food sharing (see Peterson 1993).

People did not marry members of their own band. They avoided marrying anyone they would call brother or sister. This rule was respected to such an extent that, for example, when a man who had come to the family from another band became a widower, his in-laws would start addressing him with a new term meaning "the husband of my deceased daughter." The new term publicly acknowledged that the individual was no longer a relative and could marry again inside the group.

In the old times, a widower or widow from a different band was expected to marry a younger sister or brother of the deceased spouse. If he or she did, in-laws would again address the individual with the regular kin term after the marriage. The Toba have an elaborate system of bereavement terms that reflects the force of these social practices (Mendoza and Browne 1995). Their kin terms also reflect what anthropologists call the "bilaterality" of families: neither father's nor mother's side was predominant over the other side of the family.

BAND TERRITORIES

To the subsistence of the hunter-gatherer societies of the western Chaco, annual variation in the availability of vegetables was more important than the variation in game and fish (see Gould 1991). The scattered and not-always-predictable occurrence of natural resources required that the areas exploited by different groups not only changed from season to season, but also overlapped.

Anthropologists maintain that hunter-gatherer societies have unrestricted access to natural resources. In fact, hunting and gathering grounds that over-lapped and interlocked in all directions could not advantageously have been owned by any particular group. Until today, every indigenous family has had unrestricted access to any piece of Toba land.

Habitual exploitation of the same area is what accounts for the notion of "band territory" postulated here. Members of Toba bands knew the extent of the area habitually used by each group. However, other bands would hunt and gather there if they needed to. They could also camp in the areas habitually trekked by a band that had became diminished in size due to epidemic disease, attacks by soldiers, migration to work for the white men, or other causes. In those cases, the others would acknowledge that "this place is not ours, such-and-such used to live here, but they can't now."

The people used the same notion of territory to deal with other ethnic groups, and with criollo ranchers as well. Wichí and Pilagá bands could camp in areas exploited by Toba bands, but it was expected that they would ask permission (see Spielmann 1986). In the early 1900s Toba bands per-mitted criollo ranchers to pasture their cattle in areas where the Toba habitually trekked. The ranchers agreed to give some kind of compensation to the bands.

The families chose a site because it had water and food, good land for planting, good clay for pots, or river shells to make spoons, ornaments, and other implements. If they liked the spot, they would return the next season.

When two or more bands used resources of the same area, they would not camp exactly in the same spot, except for overnight camping. If two bands camped nearby at the same time of the year, the individuals would visit each other during the day, but they remained apart. Each of these "habitual users" named the place with different names. At the beginning of my interviews, I was confused by the use of different names to identify the same place. Then I realized that each individual was recalling the places from the perspective of his or her own band.

Toba oral tradition repeats several stories about how the old leaders formed coalitions to attack Wichí and Nivaclé bands and drive them away from valuable spots on both sides of the river. The "conquered" places were usually sites with abundant water, *algarroba* beans, and game. The Toba bands that participated in such raids would later use the place as a seasonal campsite.

To reconstruct the areas where each band used to trek, I asked band members about the places where they usually camped during one annual cycle.

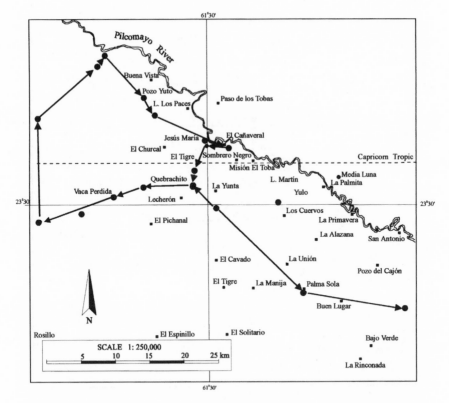

Map 6. Routes Followed by the Piogodipi (Inland) during Their Seasonal Foraging

Many Toba adults can still remember some itineraries followed by their own bands in the late 1920s. In several cases, these "travel schemes" go back and forth, from south to north, drawing a zigzag shape. (See maps 6, 7, and 8.) The people gave me either the Toba name, the Spanish name, or both for each place where bands used to camp along their seasonal itinerary. The Spanish name (which has been given by criollo ranchers in recent times) is the one that I was able to locate in the maps. The Spanish name usually relates to the meaning of the indigenous name.

The information shows that bands followed a pattern of exploiting the resources consistently and returning to the same places. I checked these data with the genealogies of band members to obtain a clue about the time when the people had been there. Then I compared my data with the data recorded by De la Cruz (1995) among the same people.[4] As a result, I have been able to obtain a reliable reconstruction of the territories of the bands.

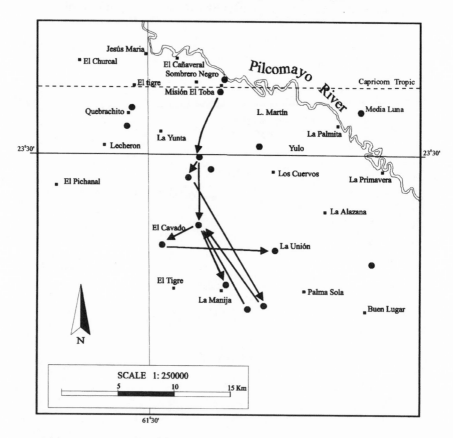

Map 7. Routes Followed by the Pegadipi (Central) during Their Seasonal Foraging

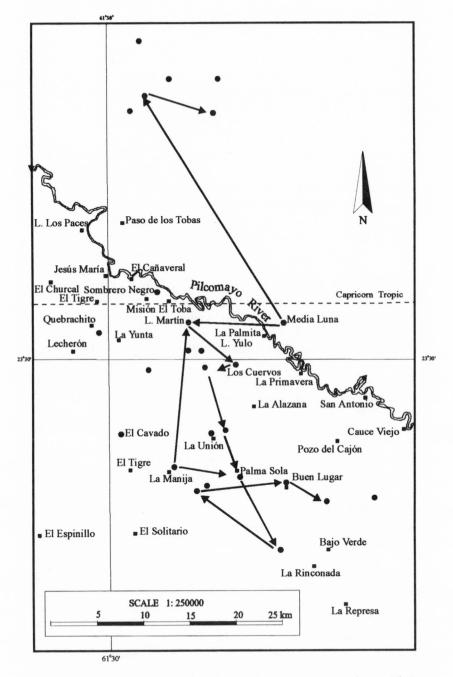

Map 8. Routes Followed by the Chiyagadipi (Downstream) during Their
Seasonal Foraging

SEASONAL ECONOMIC ACTIVITY OF BANDS

In the early 1900s the management of the environment where the Western Toba lived depended on (a) the Pilcomayo River cycle and (b) the availability of inland water. Until 1974 the people adjusted many of their seasonal economic activities to the periodic cycle of the river.[5] A few permanent inland water sources, such as lagoons and water holes, were more predictable, and for that reason the people knew their locations.

Fish, plants, and animals found in large quantities in certain localities during short periods would drive several bands to such localities (for example, fish, rheas, *pichi* [*Burmeistería retusa*, a kind of prairie dog], and *algarroba* fruits). Bands exploited the abundant resources in small groups and shared the products with neighbors and relatives. If there was any surplus, they could build a storage bin on site or carry a limited amount to trade with another group; at least since the late 1800s, some Toba bands have employed mules to carry surplus and supplies from one place to another (Thouar 1891:89).

At that time the annual cycle of economic activity was slightly different for bands living inland from those that spent the winter season near the Pilcomayo. Inland bands had their winter camps far away from river banks, while riverine bands did it the other way around. If they had stored enough food, riverine bands would remain near the river all year round. At the most, they would set camps within a two or three days' walk of the river.

In times of scarcity, riverine bands would visit Wichí villages to trade smoked and dried fish for maize and other vegetables or goods. They would also trade with families of criollo ranchers. Bands living inland would trek further north and south of the river, exploiting more diverse patches. They would trade with other indigenous groups and with the criollos, but they would exchange rhea feathers and animal skins instead of fish.

The bands would set their camps (a) in open field sites near bushes (*campos*), scrub forests, and jungles (*montes, montes fuertes*) or near lagoons, swamps, marshes (*lagunas, madrejones*), and water holes (*pozos*); (b) in creek beds and ravines (*cañadas, zanjas*); and (c) on riverbanks. All temporary campsites along the route had some provision for water.

The people would spend much of the time in camps placed along creeks, ravines, and lagoons. In the past, the Toba fought with Wichí and Nivaclé bands to control the most sheltered creeks. As these were much-traveled areas, some creeks are recalled as places of epidemic diseases. Others were considered the residence of dangerous spirits. Elders remember that in some creeks people would find remains of old pottery and ornaments unknown to them. Creeks close to the river had reed grasses and canes utilized to make arrows. Creeks close to scrub forests were considered rich in edible plants, while creeks and ravines located inland had valuable *algarrobo* trees and were chosen as sites to organize feasts and perform ceremonies.

The sites for longer stays were hunting fields (*campos altos*) that never flooded. Most of the battlefields that the Toba remember—where they fought against Argentine soldiers—are located in open field sites.

The Toba traveled through scrub forests only on well-known trails because forests and bushes were places without water. Hunters had to carry their own supply of water. Men would enter the forest to hunt prey they had already tracked down and then return to camp the same day. Women would enter the forest to gather a particular vegetable, but they would not stay there for a long time. These places were also recalled as residences of dangerous spirits.

Inland bands planted their gardens in spots that provided humidity and protection for seeds. The Toba said that in the old days there were no cows or goats to eat up the sprouts; they also said that their people would not take another person's labor without permission. The cases of hostility and revenge between members of different bands that I recorded from oral tradition, not related to adultery and witchcraft, are connected to the stealing of fruits stored in bins. To explain how bands sustained themselves in those years, I will describe the economic activities that were repeated seasonally, following the natural rhythm of availability and scarcity, as recalled by the Toba.

ECONOMIC ACTIVITY DURING HUNGRY SEASON

The worst part of the year used to be the end of winter and the beginning of spring (August–September). August is described as a period of silence (no winds), coldness, dryness, and hunger. People would trek the land in search of honey and small prey. When they saw Venus (the morning star) in the sky, it was the signal to hunt *pichi*. They also hunted iguana, rhea, peccary, deer, and smaller game. Birds were difficult to find because they were nesting at that time. Women would gather reeds, tubers, lianas, prickly pears, palm cores, rhizomes of *chaguar* (*Bromelia*), and other vegetables. The women considered these as "emergency foods."

By August, winter frosts had already damaged the most palatable fruits. The families that had stored vegetables (either cultivated or those ethnobotanists call "protected"; see Maranta 1987:197) would go back to their bins and check if there was anything left. The women cooked the available tubers and roots with vegetable salt and wild chili and dipped them into fat obtained from fish and mammals (the fat was kept in skin bags and clay pots). In muddy lagoons, the people found eels, small fish that "taste like mud," and a few other "tasteless" fish that "helped feed" the family.

At this time of the year (from June to August), the shamans prayed for rain. Folks from different bands usually gathered together to play a ball game resembling hockey, dance, and drink a fermented beverage made of honey. They also organized war parties against neighboring ethnic groups. The women would encourage their husbands to participate in a raid, in part because the women overestimated the amount of food available at their neighbors' villages. Their rationale was that their neighbors were enjoying abundance while their own children were hungry, and the mothers didn't have enough to feed them. During the dry season, war parties could travel faster and cover longer distances.

In September, *chañar* (*Geoffroea decorticans*) trees started flowering. By the end of the month, some rain would fall. The first rain was called *napeta-ganá* (the one that makes seeds grow). Some families would prepare the soil for planting squash, watermelon, corn, and tobacco. They would choose either suitable spots close to rivers or creeks with permanent water supply, or humid and low inland fields. The women gathered wild beans, fruits, and seeds. Often in September, the hot north winds produced fires. During these natural fires, people would find shelter in creeks and lagoons. After a fire, they would collect the small animals they found burned in the fields; they also organized hunting groups for rhea, deer, and other prey.

ECONOMIC ACTIVITY DURING RAINY SEASON

In October it rained and the temperature rose, but without mosquitoes yet. Fruit trees started producing again. By the end of the month, the people would be able to produce a fermented beverage from *chañar* fruits. November was a month of expectation because the women wondered if there would be enough *algarroba* (*Prosopis*) fruits. Hot temperatures stimulated its growth, but too much rain would make the fruit rotten. The women prepared big string bags and organized gathering groups. At the peak of *algarroba* season (December), men also became involved in handling the beans. Bands moved to places where the *algarrobo* trees were abundant. Several bands would camp in the same *algarrobal*, and then they would invite each other to drinking feasts. Men used to say that they worked hard searching for prey in winter, but when the fruits were ripening, it was their time to rest. The women did most of the work.

In December the river ran full, carrying "pregnant" fish, tree trunks, and other materials from the mountains. The riverine bands did not fish at this time, but consumed dry fish kept in storage. By the end of the month, the river flooded and riverine bands moved to elevated (dry) places. Frogs, toads, and turtles could be heard singing at night. Rays appeared in the water, along with piranhas, a kind of otter, capybaras, and other animals. Inland bands preferred to fish in ponds and water holes filled by the flooding and heavy rains. Water birds also came to fish in the lagoons, and they were caught with traps.

In January and part of February the river was still in full flow. Men fished individually from the riverbanks because the waters ran too fast and

2. Mother and daughter carry home the collection

became dangerous. They shot fish with bow and arrow and with harpoon. At this time, they referred to fish with a word that means "fish are sprouting" (like leaves sprouting from a branch). Fish was not the main food during the rainy season because it was considered lean and tasteless. At this time of the year, folks were invited to each other's villages to gamble and drink.

During the summer, inland people had plenty of food: bush animals had already produced offspring, bees had made some honey, and vegetables were abundant. In every village, women stored dry vegetables in bins. By the end of February, the families who had planted successful gardens were able to share their crops. Some families would try to plant squash and pumpkin for the second time at the end of February.

In March and April the riverine bands trekked inland, while the fishermen prepared their nets for winter fishing. The families camped at locations where they found good clay to make pots (they would need the pots to store the fat from fish). Water from swamps and marshes started to recede. Caimans could be hunted in the river. There were still many edible plants available. Butterflies and flies appeared in the camps. They were welcome because the old people said that an abundance of flies meant that a lot of fish would come from downriver.

3. A *caraguatá* bag in the making

WINTER FISHING

May and June were the peak of the fishing season. When word that fish were ascending the rivers spread, all bands would travel to the riverbanks. They would camp at separate spots to enjoy the abundance of meat. Inland bands, either Toba or Wichí, that had ties with bands camped near the riverbank would make arrangements with those riverine bands to fish at the best fishing sites. Among the many fishermen who joined the winter fishing, some would cooperate, while others would fish alone.

People had learned to understand the behavior of fish as much as they understood the behavior of other living beings. Toba fishermen referred to what they did to drive the schools of fish into their nets as if they were talking about managing a flock of peccaries or rhea. They used to place fences of branches inside the water, parallel to the shore, and drive the schools there. At night, one or two men with long sticks would beat the water at one end of the narrowing lane along the shore,[6] and the fishermen with dip nets would catch the frightened fish at the other end of the line. The beaters always received a share of the fish that were caught. During the daylight, old men and boys would make a barrier in the water along the shore with large barring nets, trying to catch as much as they could, while experienced fishermen would fish with dip nets. They would also walk in teams, barring the water downstream to get the fish that were migrating upstream. Métraux (1946a:252) wrote, "There is scant discipline in these communal drives, and everyone stops fishing at his own will."

During the peak of the season, fish were so abundant that the families were able to store not only dried and smoked fish, but also the fat of cooked fish. They built little storage huts (similar to bins) to store dried fish on layers of a kind of grass that prevented the decomposition of dried meat. At this time, men did not hunt much "because they had a strong fish smell" that the animals would not like, although they collected the vegetables used as salt to make the meat tasteful. Women kept busy cooking, smoking, and drying fish.

As the Toba had to be up all night to take advantage of the abundance of fish, they gathered to talk, smoke, and watch the stars. The Toba have names and stories for many of the stars they watch in the winter firmament (from June to September). They say that stars seem to be distant and less visible in summer. At dawn, old people would speak to Dapitchí (see Tomasini 1976) to request that he have compassion on them and not send freezing cold weather. By the end of July, the constellation of Pleiades became invisible for a few days from the latitude of the Tropic of Capricorn where the Toba live.

4. A fish roast with stew in the making

5. Drinking *mate* and listening to music

They said that Dapitchí was gone (see Pérez Diez 1974:118). This event sig-naled the change of seasons from abundance to scarcity. The Toba called this event *conajagañi loñi* (the turn that makes us suffer and brings frost).

In July those families that had planted a new garden in summer would be able to gather some squash and pumpkins. From July to August, cold south winds lowered temperatures and the water became extremely cold. Inland bands went back to fish in lagoons and ponds where numb fish were easily caught with fishnets and spears. People who remained on the riverbanks used to build wooden platforms on quiet river bends. They placed a layer of dirt on top of the platforms so they could burn a fire to keep warm at night while fishing with a dip net. At night, too, they would fish in depressions and holes of the riverbed where the numb fish found shelter. Experienced fishermen, with their bodies covered by fish fat to maintain body tempera-ture, could dive into the water with barring nets and return to the surface with their catch. Then the fishermen would hurry to warm themselves by the fires set along the banks. They said that no one could dive into the cold wa-ters more than two times in the same night. Today old men exhibit as tro-phies the scars of piranha bites they got from diving into cold deep water. At this time of the year, neighboring Nivaclé bands might built zigzag weirs or dams to catch fish from their own platforms (Tomasini 1978–79:87). In those cases, the Toba bands along the river organized war raids to destroy the dams.

MEN AND WOMEN IN FAMILY LIFE

Traditionally, Toba men considered themselves to be strong and courageous individuals. They were able to impose respect, even fear, on neighboring indigenous groups and on criollo settlers. Toba women were equally
respected, and sometimes feared, by men. Toba parents have been raising
and educating durable and self-confident children for generations. For example, the adults still remember the many "tests of endurance" planned by
their parents, in which the children had to prove that they were able to walk
barefooted on hot soil, carry heavy weights, endure thirst, run fast through
thorny trails, and the like.

Each male activity (economic, religious, or political) in Toba society has
had its counterpart in the female domain, except the role of warrior. The
men contributed with meat and honey to the household, but the women
provided vegetables, water, and wood to keep the fires alive. Men and
women performed as shamans, although only women were viewed as
"witches." The wives of leaders were as influential inside communities as
their husbands.

In particular, youngsters who expressed a desire to participate in raids
against enemies were taught indigenous strategies for surprise attacks. When
they grew older, they were initiated as warriors. The planning of a war raid
was a serious matter: leaders met to discuss their actions, shamans had to
make sure that the occasion was appropriate, and warriors danced and prayed
that they might achieve victory. Karsten (1923:17) wrote about the strategies
for war of Bolivian Toba: "The Indians in their wars do not act like a disorga-
nized mob, but work on carefully-planned lines. Some men are sent out as
spies with the object of coming as near the enemy as possible and getting all
the intelligence about him they can. In their actions they exercise the greatest
prudence, rarely fighting in a body and trying to overthrow the enemy with as
little loss of life as possible." The most common reason to organize a party
used to be getting revenge for a previous offense. Women themselves encouraged their husbands and fathers to participate in such war parties.

Women did not take part in rituals of preparation for war (like the "dance
of courage," Métraux 1937:395) or in the raid itself. Sexual contact with a
woman before the raid would endanger the performance of a warrior. Yet
women were involved in the distribution of the booty. Little children who
had been taken as captives would be raised by the women as if they were
children of their own. However, women from other ethnic groups taken as
captives by the warriors might encounter rejection and hardship from the
Toba women of the villages (see Henry and Henry 1944:13).

In the oral tradition, Toba women appear anxiously waiting for the arrival
of a war party. Older men recall the scene of unmarried young women coming to receive war trophies when the party approached the village. It was the
beginning of a ritual ceremony. The women would take the scalps and heads
of enemies to the center of the village and denigrate and ridicule them (Arnott

1934:316). Then the warriors would perform "the dance of the scalps." Women collected the fruits to prepare the fermented beverage employed to celebrate. During the feast itself, the women and a few designated warriors did not drink. Chervin (1908:135) wrote: "Each tribe has some warriors who never drink and who have the task of appeasing quarrels. The women are all very temperate." Older women said that they remained sober to be able to take care of those who had lost their minds to the beverage.

INTERNAL CONTROL OF AGGRESSION

Traditionally, the Toba have restrained the expression of physical violence between persons. What I refer to here as "physical violence" and "aggression" follow closely the Toba definition of events. The actors would say that they got involved in a "fight," an "attack," or a "revenge." The initiator of this kind of event was always motivated by an intense personal feeling of anger, disappointment, or even madness. Anthropologist Victoria Burbank (1994) has taken a similar position in her analysis of anger and aggression among Australian aboriginal women.

The advice "do not fight with your kin" has been present in the public discourse of leaders for a long time. Métraux (1937:397) quoted the words of a chief spoken at the beginning of a feast: "Drink, he told them, but it is not necessary to quarrel; avoid violence and insults. Drink tranquilly, let no one get angry. Our ancestors taught us to drink, but they did not give us the beer so that we would wrangle. Take *aloja* and eat your fill, but do not quarrel!" The people expect their leaders to be able to intervene in internal disputes and stop all physical violence between band members. Toba parents transmit the same advice to their children today.

In Toba playgroups, children viewed as leaders by their peers display the same attitude expected from adult leaders. In particular, children who exhibit attitudes of leadership in Toba playgroups will (a) lead the activities, deciding alone what the group will do; (b) "impose" their will over dissenting opinions; (c) cooperate and share with the most vulnerable members of the group; and (d) correct "deviant" behavior. The last two features have not been described as common traits of leadership among children of other cultures. They do not appear, for example, in studies of children's behavior in playgroups of the urban middle class in the United States (Perry, Perry, and Rasmussen 1986; Sackin and Thelen 1984).

GENDER DIFFERENCES IN THE EXPRESSION OF PHYSICAL AGGRESSION

Toba men express aggression differently in public than they do in private. When two men fight in the presence of others, the confrontation takes a ritualized form that follows a cultural pattern. The purpose of this form of "ritualized beating" is to express a contender's aggressive feelings without harming the other. For example, the opponents would measure their mutual strength by holding each other tightly and pushing each other with open hands, but they would never use their fists or arms to cause injury to an opponent. The individual who could endure the most pressure was considered the victorious contestant. The social situations that might motivate this kind of ritual aggression between men include serious disagreements of opinion in the process of making a decision that affects the families involved, accusations of dishonesty or sorcery, extramarital affairs of a wife, and incestuous relations of a female close kin.

In cases where two men engage in a "ritualized beating" in a public place, other men do not intervene to stop the fight. The common explanation is that they respect the desire of the individuals confronting each other. However, the presence of relatives provides a frame of restraint for the contenders. Interestingly, the contenders may accept the intervention of a closely related woman to end their ritualized confrontation (De la Cruz 1994). The fact that Toba women act as mediators in public situations of male ritualized aggression indicates the amount of female influence in the everyday life of communities.

When two men engage in a ritualized fight, and neither of the opponents is able to impose himself over the other, the individual who has initiated the fight may decide to let the other go. He might decide that he is already appeased and will not fight for the same reason again. Moreover, two men who want to resolve their differences by fighting can decide to confront each other at a secluded place away from the villages. They might come to that meeting place carrying a weapon. In the past, they would also paint their faces in red and wear war ornaments. Such private "duels" usually end with at least one of the contenders wounded.

In contrast, Toba women fight violently among themselves in public places. Their people do not sanction them if they decide to solve their differences through physical aggression. None of the men around the contenders try to stop a fight between women, even if one of the opponents is a close relative (mother, sister, daughter, or wife).

Fights among women have been recorded many times by previous authors (O. Leake 1932:93; W. Leake 1933:114; Métraux 1937:385–386). For example, Chervin (1908:131) wrote: "The women are very jealous of each other; on the slightest pretext they come to blows. A Toba can repudiate his wife, but it is impossible for him to have two spouses at the same time; they would beat each other to death. Naked to the waist, a jaguar skin firmly attached to their loins, they fight in the center of the *ranchería*, surrounded by their partisans, their wrists armed with very sharp fish or goat bones, and they attack each other's chest and body. The men, impassive, watch the fight until one of the two succumbs to the blows of her enemy, or the other pulls off her jaguar skin. The stripped one flees, ashamed, amid the whoops and cries of the bystanders." Authors have recorded also the special weapons used by women in their fights. Nordenskiöld (1919:53) called them "knuckle-dusters." They were made of wood or hide; sometimes a knuckle-duster could include piranha teeth, inserted to make them even more harmful.

Two women would fight because one of them was offended by the other's accusation of egoism, greediness, or defamation; or because their children had quarreled before; or the goats of one family entered the garden of the other's family. Above all, a woman would confront another if she knew that the other woman was having an extramarital affair with her husband. In these latter cases, the female relatives of the offended woman, who also knew the situation, expected her to react with violence. The woman's female relatives would themselves engage in a fight with the relatives of the offender. The woman who planned to fight another woman prepared herself by tying up her hair, rolling up her skirt or dress, and removing necklaces and ornaments. If she wanted to cause real harm to her opponent, she would also carry a weapon.

Missionary William Price (1933:81) wrote about this subject as follows: "It is amazing how one's ideas have to be readjusted on the mission field. In the great stories, poems, epics and romances of civilized countries, it is generally the men who fight over the woman they love. Here the opposite holds good. A few nights ago we were called upon to interfere in a fight between two women over a man who had apparently deserted both of them in turn. Each combatant was supported by the female population of her respective village, and a large crowd had gathered together to witness the contest. Sitting on logs near the fire or reclining on blankets were the men, evidently enjoying the prospect of a good fight."

When two women who are close kin (a mother and a daughter or two sisters, for example) want to express anger and disappointment, they may engage in a "ritualized beating," similar to that of men. Standing one in front of one another, they push each other with open hands and struggle, shouting offensive expressions to each other, but they do not cause any harm to themselves. This kind of ritualized expression of aggression usually ends with the intervention of another woman.

GENDER DIFFERENCES IN THE EXPRESSION OF CHILD AGGRESSION

Toba children, like any other children, begin their socialization process reproducing what they learn from their caregivers (Tronick, Morelli, and Winn 1987:98). As they mature, children learn to accommodate their behavior to the cultural expectations of their group (Draper and Harpending 1987).

Anthropologists and missionaries have often reported their impressions about how indigenous children reproduce the behavior of adults in their common social interactions. For example, at a time when the Toba and neighboring groups were still engaged in internal wars, Nordenskiöld (1912:60) wrote about the behavior of Nivaclé children: "When the Nivaclé Indians were at war with the Toba, the children of the Nivaclé villages used to play war. They divided themselves into two gangs, one representing the Nivaclé and the other representing the Toba. The arms were fragments of canes; shouts and howls accompanied the combat. The gang who took a prisoner scalped him; while one or two of the children supported the head of the prisoner, another child made the movement as if he were to strip the skin from the head. Moreover, I have seen children dividing themselves into two groups, one representing the Whites and the other representing the Indians. Even in their most violent games, I have never witnessed a trace of brutality" (my translation).

The authors who studied the behavior of children among Chaco indigenous groups (for example, Henry and Henry 1944) have mentioned the absence of serious physical aggression between playmates. However, observers noted that Toba girls could express physical aggression more freely than boys. For example, Métraux (1937:385) noticed: "I recall having seen little girls line up in two rows to practice giving each other blows with the fist as they see their mothers and elder sisters doing."

Different patterns of aggressive and prosocial behavior pass down from one generation to the next as the children learn to accommodate to the expectations of the adults in their respective communities (Fry 1988:1009). Gender differences in aggression are less a matter of competence, because girls and boys see themselves as roughly equal in capacity for aggression, than a matter of performance. For example, compared to boys, American urban middle-class girls (Perry, Perry, and Rasmussen 1986:703) expected more disapproval from both peers and themselves for behaving aggressively. Girls had internalized cultural proscriptions against aggression; they also expected to be less successful than boys in securing rewards. In the Toba case, expression of female children's physical aggression is not proscribed by the adult community.

In my own recorded observations of the behavior of Toba children in playgroups, boys engaged in agonistic behavior more often than girls. Examples of young male agonistic behavior in Toba playgroups are (a) menacing with an extended arm (either with an open hand or with a fist, or shaking an object), accompanying the gesture with a strong look and a facial expression of anger; and (b) standing in front of another individual, moving the upper body up and down (as in a "cock fight"), with eyes sharply focused on the opponent's face. However, the girls actually engaged in physical aggression more often than boys. I recorded "physical aggression" in playgroups when I observed, for example, a child who intended to cause harm to another child by hitting his or her body with an object or by damaging or taking away something that the other had been using (an object, food, or the like). This difference has proven to be statistically significant

(Mendoza 1994:234). In my observations, girls tended to fight more often with younger girls or with girls of about the same age.

A typical sequence of physical aggression among Toba children seven years old and younger observed in a playgroup situation would be as follows: (*a*) one child attacks his or her playmate; (*b*) the aggrieved child immediately reacts (cries, hits back, directs a strong look at the aggressor, or the like); (*c*) a third individual, usually an older child, intervenes. The "mediator" either removes the aggrieved child or the object employed by his or her aggressor and then comforts the aggrieved child, completely ignoring the behavior of the one who initiated the aggression. The child who has been attacked does not offer conciliatory gestures to the aggressor.

Submissive behavior does not appear in the termination of aggressive interactions among Toba children. However, researchers of child aggressive behavior maintain that conciliatory and submissive gestures, which are the most common forms of conflict resolution in the observations of playgroups of American preschoolers, help to maintain the hierarchy of dominance within a group. Researchers have also studied how altruism, leadership, and aid-giving behavior help to maintain a "dominance hierarchy" in groups of school-age American children.

Anthropologists have not published systematic observational evidence on dominance hierarchies among children in foraging societies. Nevertheless, the consensus of anthropological studies indicates that these hierarchies are less important among foragers than in other societies. Systematic observational studies of common aggressive situations in hunter-gatherer communities may challenge our traditional views about the adaptive value of males as more aggressive than females. In foraging societies, individuals have such an important degree of social interdependence and face-to-face relationships that maintaining a straightforward view of the meaning of aggression (for example, males compete for females or for hierarchical positions) might be highly misleading (see Blurton-Jones and Konner 1973).

CONCLUSION

Anthropologists like Palavecino (1939) and Métraux (1937, 1946a), who addressed the subsistence economy of the Western Toba before the 1950s, did not explain how the bands used the resources of land nor how the families actually organized their seasonal foraging. The materials discussed in the first part of this chapter refer specifically to these issues as they have been kept in Toba oral tradition from a time that goes back to the period when the mentioned anthropologists conducted their fieldwork.

The materials discussed under the heading "Men and Women in Family Life" in some way intend to respond to an unformulated question: what happened to the warriors? My discussion of the forms of internal control of aggression among adults suggests that Toba society offers "ritualized" channels through which members can channel strong emotions and resolve disruptive confrontations. I believe that the mere existence of these channels is connected with the fact that a "war complex" was prevalent in Toba society three generations ago. In other words, in a society where warriors were valued members whose aggressive behavior received positive sanction (in a society where killing enemies in war enhanced the status of warriors), the existence of cultural channels to manage internal physical aggression was important to maintain concord among individuals.

My study about how Toba children express their aggression today suggests that current patterns of the socialization process still reflect the manner in which adults control aggressive behaviors among themselves. My point is that the recent shift toward sedentarism made by Toba people and the adoption of new forms of economic subsistence have not changed substantially this specific feature. This modality of the socialization process of Toba children corresponds to what some authors refer to as "the population's modal personality" of hunter-gatherer societies (see Kelly 1995:329).

Additionally, my brief discussion of the attitudes of leadership exhibited by Toba children in playgroups addresses another unformulated question: what happened to the leaders? I have studied this subject elsewhere (Mendoza 1998), but my observation here is consistent with the previous one. I have the strong impression that two or three generations of immersion into the Argentine nation-state have not actually transformed the egalitarian characteristics of Toba indigenous society.

NOTES

1. I carried out fieldwork among the Western Toba in 1984, 1985, 1987, 1988, and 1993–95. My research has been supported by grants and fellowships from the National Council for Scientific and Technological Research (CONICET), Argentina, and a Seashore Fellowship from the Graduate College of the University of Iowa. I wish to express my gratitude to the people of the Toba communities of west Formosa, Argentina, who allowed me to participate in their lives, share their memories, and report what I have learned to others.

2. For example, Pedro Lozano (1941 [1733]); Joaquín Camaño (in Furlong 1955 [1778]); and Pero Hernández (in Vivante 1943:86–87).

3. In 1905 the expedition of Argentine governor Lucas Luna Olmos reached the border of this zone coming from downstream. Luna Olmos reported (1949:44): "This region is a battlefield; none of the Indians would live here" (my translation).

4. Most of the 165 sites I recorded during fieldwork correspond to those recorded by De la Cruz, except for sites located in the Paraguayan Chaco, which I have not been able to situate in printed maps.

5. In December 1974 and January 1975 the Pilcomayo River flooded to such an unusual extent that the flooding destroyed several Toba villages and the Toba Anglican Mission near the criollo hamlet of Sombrero Negro. Since then the Toba have relocated their settlements south of the river course, which is now swamps and marshland.

6. The beaters of the team have been described as "goalkeepers" and the fenced lane as a kind of gangplank like the one criollo ranchers employ to drive cows into a corral.

REFERENCES

Arnott, J. 1934. Los Toba-Pilagá del Chaco y sus guerras. *Revista Geográfica Americana* 1(7): 491–501.

Astrada, D. 1906. *Expedición al Pilcomayo: Colonización del Alto Chaco*, Buena Ventura, la expedición, tierras, caminos, antecedentes (17 de junio a 24 septiembre 1903). Buenos Aires: Robles y Cía.

Baldrich, J. A. 1889. *Las comarcas vírgenes: El Chaco Central Norte*. Buenos Aires: Imprenta Jacobo Peuser.

Blurton-Jones, N. G., and M. J. Konner. 1973. Sex Differences in Behaviour of London and Bushman Children. In: *Comparative Ecology and Behaviour of Primates*, ed. R. P. Michael and J. H. Crook, 799–828. London: Academic Press.

Burbank, Victoria K. 1994. *Fighting Women: Anger and Aggression in Aboriginal Australia*. Berkeley: University of California Press.

Campos, D. 1888. *De Tarija a la Asunción: Expedición boliviana de 1883*. Buenos Aires: Imprenta Jacobo Peuser.

Cardús, J. 1886. *Las misiones franciscanas entre los infieles de Bolivia*. Barcelona: Librería de la Inmaculada Concepción.

Chervin, A. 1908. *Anthropologie bolivienne*. Paris: Imprimerie Nationale. Vol. 1, "Tobas," pp.129–139. [English translation by F. Schütze: *The Toba*. New Haven, Conn.: HRAF 1981].

Cordini, I. R. 1947. *Los ríos Pilcomayo en la región del Patiño*. Anales 1. Buenos Aires: Secretaría de Industria y Comercio, Dirección de Minas y Geología.

De la Cruz, Luís. 1989. La situación de ocupación territorial de las comunidades aborígenes del Chaco Salteño y su tratamiento legal. *Suplemento Antropológico* 24(2): 87–144.

———. 1994. Personal communication.

———. 1995. Qomlajépi naleua, nuestra tierra: Los sitios que contienen la tierra que da vida a los tobas de Sombrero Negro de la provincia de Formosa. *Hacia Una Nueva Carta Étnica del Gran Chaco* 5:69–115.

De la Cruz, Luís, and M. Mendoza. 1989. Les Tobas de l'ouest de Formosa et le processus de reconnaissance légale de la propriété communautaire des terres. *Recherches Amerindiennes au Quebec* 19(4): 43–51.

Draper, P., and H. Harpending. 1987. Parent Investment and the Child's Environment. In *Parenting across the Life Span: Biosocial Dimensions*, ed. J. Lancaster, J. Altmann, A. Rossi, and L. Sherrod, 207–235. New York: Aldine.

Fry, D. P. 1988. Intercommunity Differences in Aggression among Zapotec Children. *Child Development* 59:1008–1019.

Furlong, G.S.J. 1955. *Joaquín Camaño, S. J., y su "Noticia del Gran Chaco" (1778)*. Buenos Aires: Librería del Plata.

Gordillo, G. 1995. La subordinación y sus mediaciones: Dinámica cazadora-recolectora, relaciones de producción, capital comercial y estado entre los tobas del oeste de Formosa. In *Producción doméstica y capital: Estudios desde la antropología económica*, ed. H. Trinchero, 105–138. Buenos Aires: Biblos.

Gould, R. A. 1991. Arid-Land Foraging as Seen from Australia: Adaptive Models and Behavioral Realities. *Oceania* 62(1): 12–33.

Henry, J., and Z. Henry. 1944. *Doll Play of Pilagá Indian Children: An Experimental and Field Analysis of the Behavior of the Pilagá Indian Children*. Research Monograph No. 4. American Orthopsychiatric Association, Inc.

Karsten, R. 1923. *The Toba Indians of the Bolivian Gran Chaco*. Acta Academiae Aboensis Humaniora 4. Abo, Finland: Abo Akademi.

———. 1932. *Indian Tribes of the Argentine and Bolivian Chaco*. Ethnological Studies. Commentationes Humanarum Litterarum, 4, 1. Helsingfors: Akademische Buchhandlung.

Kelly, R. L. 1995. *The Foraging Spectrum: Diversity in Hunter-Gatherer Lifeways*. Washington, D.C.: Smithsonian Institution Press.

Koch, T. 1902. Die Guaikúrustämme III/IV: Toba. *Globus* 81:69–78, 105–112 [English translation by F. Schütze: *The Guaikuru Tribe*. New Haven, Conn.: HRAF 1980].

Leake, O. 1932. Toba Mission Staff Notes. *South American Missionary Society Magazine* (London), February–April, 93–94.

Leake, W. A. 1933. The Warlike Ways of Toba Women. *South American Missionary Society Magazine* (London), September–December, 114–116.

Lozano, Pedro. 1941. *Descripción corográfica del Gran Chaco Gualamba*. San Miguel de Tucumán: Universidad de Tucumán.

Luna Olmos, L. 1949. *Expedición al río Pilcomayo en 1905*. Formosa: Policía de Territorios.

Maranta, A. 1987. Los recursos vegetales alimenticios de la etnia Mataco del Chaco Centro Occidental. *Parodiana* 5(1): 161–237.

Mendoza, M. 1994. Técnicas de observación directa para estudiar interacciones sociales infantiles entre los Toba. *Runa* 21:241–262.

———. 1998. Authority and Respect among the Toba of Northwest Argentina: Politics, Leadership, and History (1870–1995). Typescript.

Mendoza, M., and M. Browne. 1995. Términos de parentesco y términos de duelo de los Tobas del oeste de Formosa. *Hacia Una Nueva Carta Étnica del Gran Chaco* 6:117–122.

Métraux, A. 1937. Etudes d'ethnographie Toba-Pilagá (Gran Chaco). *Anthropos* 32:171–194, 378–401 [English translation by F. Schütze: *Studies of Toba-Pilagá Ethnography*. New Haven, Conn.: HRAF 1980].

———. 1946a. Ethnography of the Chaco. In *Handbook of South American Indians*, ed. J. H. Steward, 1:197–370. Washington, D.C.: Smithsonian Institution, Bureau of American Ethnology.

———. 1946b. *Myths of the Toba and Pilagá Indians of the Gran Chaco*. Memoirs of the American Folklore Society, 40. Philadelphia: American Folklore Society.

Miller, Elmer S. 1979. *Los Tobas argentinos: Armonía y disonancia en una sociedad*. Mexico City: Siglo XXI.

Nordenskiöld, E. 1912. *La vie des Indiens dans le Chaco (Amérique du Sud)*. Revue de Géographie, 6(3). Paris: Libraire Delagrave.

———. 1919. *An Ethno-geographical Analysis of the Material Culture of Two Indian Tribes in the Gran Chaco*. Göteborg: Elanders Boktryckeri Aktiebolag.

Palavecino, E. 1928. Las tribus aborígenes del Chaco Occidental. *Anales de la Sociedad Argentina de Estudios Geográficos* 3(1): 186–209.

————. 1939. Las culturas aborígenes del Chaco. In *Historia de la nación Argentina: Desde los orígenes hasta la organización definitiva en 1862*, dir. R. Levene, 1:387–417. Buenos Aires: El Ateneo-Academia Nacional de la Historia.

————. 1942. Investigaciones etnográficas y antropológicas en el Chaco Salteño. *Revista del Museo de La Plata* 16 (n.s.): 59–64.

Pérez Diez, A. A. 1974. Noticia sobre la concepción del ciclo anual entre los Matacos del Noreste de Salta. *Scripta Ethnologica* 2(2): 111–120.

Perry, D. G., L. C. Perry, and P. Rasmussen. 1986. Cognitive Social Learning Mediators of Aggression. *Child Development* 57:700–711.

Peterson, N. 1991. Cash, Commoditisation, and Authenticity: When Do Aboriginal People Stop Being Hunter-Gatherers? In *Cash, Commoditisation and Changing Foragers*, ed. N. Peterson and T. Matsuyuara, 67–90. Senri Ethnological Studies, 30. Osaka: National Museum of Ethnology.

————. 1993. Demand Sharing: Reciprocity and the Pressure for Generosity among Foragers. *American Anthropologist* 95(4): 860–874.

Price, W. J. 1933. The Tobas of Sombrero Negro. *SAMS Magazine* (London), September–December, 81.

Rýden, S. 1935. Skalpierung bei den Tobaindianern. *Etnologiska Studier* 1:26–34 [English translation by F. Schütze: *Scalping among the Toba Indians*. New Haven, Conn.: HRAF, 1980].

Sackin, S., and E. Thelen. 1984. An Ethological Study of Peaceful Associative Outcomes to Conflict in Preschool Children. *Child Development* 55:1098–1102.

Shapiro, S. 1962. The Toba Indians of Bolivia. *América Indígena* 22(3): 241–245.

Siegrist de Gentile, N. 1982. Un informe de Baldomero Cárlsen sobre la Frontera del Chaco Salteño en 1871. *Folia Histórica del Nordeste* 5:153–216.

Spielmann, K. A. 1986. Interdependence among Egalitarian Societies. *Journal of Anthropological Archaeology* 5(4): 279–312.

Tebboth, D. 1989. *With Teb: Among the Tobas: Letters Written Home from the Mission Field*. Kent, England: Lantern Press.

Thouar, A. 1891. *Explorations dans l'Amérique du Sud*. Paris: Hachette.

Tissera, R. 1972. *Chaco Gualamba: Historia de un nombre*. Resistencia, Chaco: Ediciones Cultural Nordeste.

Tomasini, A. 1976. Dapitchi, un alto dios uranio de los Toba y Pilagá. *Scripta Ethnologica* 4(1): 69–87.

————. 1978–79. Contribución al estudio de los indios Nivaklé (Chulupí) del Chaco Boreal. *Scripta Ethnologica* 5(2): 77–92.

Tronick, E. Z., G. Morelli, and S. Winn. 1987. Multiple Caretaking of Efe (Pigmy) Infants. *American Anthropologist* 89(1): 96–106.

Ventur, P. 1991. Native North American Trickster-and-Vulture Tales. In *New Dimensions in Ethnohistory*, ed. B. Gough and L. Christie, 227–268. Mercury Series Paper 120. Quebec: Canadian Museum of Civilization.

Vivante, A. 1943. *Pueblos primitivos de Sudamérica*. Buenos Aires: Emecé Editores.

6

※ ※ ───── ※ ※

Argentina's Eastern Toba: Vitalizing Ethnic Consciousness and Determination

Elmer S. Miller

From the earliest centuries of Spanish penetration into the Gran Chaco, writers documented the presence of Toba groups on the upper Pilcomayo River (Marcela Mendoza's Western Toba in chapter 5) as distinct from groups with the same name found in the lower Pilcomayo and Bermejo region, whom the Spaniards initially called Frentones (long-foreheaded ones) owing to the practice of shaving their foreheads. The latter groups, identified here as Eastern Toba, were by far the largest in number and extent.[1] While both western and eastern groups call themselves *qom* or *nam qom* (the people), the Spaniards identified them as Toba from the early centuries of contact, a name that at least some *qom* themselves adopted already in the early eighteenth century when they were communicating with the Spanish-speaking world.[2]

Most of what Mendoza states about the hunting, fishing, and gathering activities of western groups into the early twentieth century applies equally well to eastern groups. It would appear, however, that the former continue to depend to a greater extent upon foraging resources than do the latter. By the third decade of the twentieth century, immigrants from Europe and criollo settlers began to stake out significant amounts of territory occupied by Eastern Toba bands, confining them increasingly to isolated islands of existence. Meanwhile, two reservations (*reducciones de Indios*) had been demarcated for the "education" of Indians, one for Toba and Mocoví in Chaco Province at Napalpí, and another for Toba and Pilagá in Formosa Province at Bartolomé de las Casas. Only a small percentage of indigenous families could settle on these reservations, however, and many have continued to interact with kin in independent settlements throughout the region, a number of which were officially authorized by President Juan Perón in the late 1940s.

Currently there are some fifty settlements of Toba in rural areas of the eastern Chaco and Formosa provinces, plus increasingly larger and more permanent settlements in major cities, such as Resistencia, Sáenz Peña, and Formosa, not to mention Santa Fe, Rosario, and Buenos Aires. (See map 9.) In recent decades, smaller provincial Chaco cities also have acquired their own Toba barrios. Population estimates vary widely, owing partly to movement from place to place and partly to inadequate census-taking strategies. Most calculations range between thirty and forty thousand, a significant increase since my initial arrival in 1959.[3]

Map 9. Locations of Eastern Toba Settlements

6. The author with Antonio Domingo in Machagai, 1988

THE SOCIOECONOMIC CONTEXT

As the Toba increasingly lost access to game and other forest resources throughout this century, they came to rely more and more on seasonal wage labor in lumber, sugarcane, and cotton industries, supplementing their wages with various hunting, fishing, and collecting resources. When these industries came to depend less on day labor for various reasons in recent decades, and foraging resources became increasingly inaccessible, the Toba migrated in larger numbers to cities. In urban settlements, women walk the streets with carrying bags, requesting handouts from door to door, while men find sporadic day labor. A few acquire more permanent positions in small industry or municipal government. The focus of this chapter is on processes of change in the Chaco itself; the following one by Pablo Wright concentrates on Toba experiences in major urban centers.

The isolated rural settlements are comprised of band remnants living primarily on fiscal territory allotted to them originally by federal, and by the mid-twentieth century, provincial authorities. They live on extended-family plots where vegetables, and sometimes significant amounts of cotton, are grown. The families constitute segments of larger regional social categories distinguished by dialect and the geographical niche where they had roamed to exploit the primary food resources. Senior family males with shamanistic skills provided leadership by healing the sick and serving as spokesmen for interactions with the world about them. Kinship terms and marriage practices continue to reflect cognatic ties, and initial residence at marriage depends nowadays primarily upon which family of the newlyweds has available space. Urban settlements undermine traditional kinship and marriage practices by bringing together a wider range of regional acquaintances, including intermarriage with criollos.

Until the mid-twentieth century, each Toba settlement interacted independently with regional and national governmental agencies and nongovernmental organizations (NGOs). Throughout the latter half of this century, however, several developments have contributed to greater communication between regional settlements, fostering a growing sense of ethnic identity and self-determination vis-à-vis the larger society. The initial and perhaps most significant event in this regard was the formation of the indigenous Iglesia Evangélica Unida (IEU, or United Evangelical Church) in the 1950s, with its regional representation and annual conferences.

Reorganization of the Chaco and Formosa provincial Offices of Indian Affairs in the 1980s, which incorporated elected indigenous leadership, further promoted interaction and self-consciousness on a more regional basis. The formation of bilingual schools where Toba, Wichí (Mataco), and Mocoví young people are trained to teach grade school in their own languages has been the most recent contributor to the vitalization process under consideration here. Of course, interaction with criollos in urban settings impacts upon this process as well, sometimes offering opportunities for young people to abandon ties to their ethnic heritage by forming nuclear-family units that function independently, having little or no organic relationship with the extended intergenerational and collateral kin ties that persisted throughout the centuries of contact in the Chaco.

This chapter will focus primarily on the penetration of Protestant-type teachings in the form of Pentecostalism throughout the mid- to later twentieth century. The tape-recorded voices of leading participants are the primary source to illustrate the nature of Pentecostalism's impact on Toba life.[4]

INITIAL PROTESTANT MISSIONARY ACTIVITY

The first Protestant attempt to establish a presence in the Argentine Chaco was the British Emmanuel Mission, located in El Espinillo from 1934 to 1949, where a church, school, clinic, and store were established with personnel assigned to carry out these various activities.[5] The Mennonites established a mission in Aguará from 1943 to 1955 based on the same structural principles.[6] The idea of both missions was to share the gospel as the missionaries understood it, which meant instructing the Toba in reading and writing Spanish, in farming the land and managing money, in the germ theory of disease and hygiene, but above all, in public worship services involving Bible reading, prayer, and singing.

The two missions also attempted to extend their work to neighboring communities: the Emmanuel Mission to bands along the Bermejo river; the Mennonites to Legua 15 and Legua 17. Both ran into personnel problems that included disagreement over how best to carry out their assignments, but more important, they encountered little enthusiasm among the Toba for the gospel message as they defined it. There were some successful "conversions," and several individuals seemed to get the hang of the catechism. However, missionaries encountered little resonance in Toba culture for the message itself, little genuine excitement about the overall approach. Both missions disbanded in considerable frustration that included a sense of failure: the Emmanuel Mission involuntarily, protesting official opposition from a priest and local authorities; the Mennonites voluntarily, basing their decision upon the evaluation of an invited anthropologist.[7]

Meanwhile, Pentecostal missions were finding greater resonance for their message in the 1940s. The Church of God Pentecostal in Buenos Aires authorized Chief Pedro Martínez to travel throughout the Chaco and appoint local *culto* leaders, while Go Ye Mission in Resistencia and Grace and Glory Mission in El Zapallar extended their outreach to the Toba as well. The Foursquare Gospel Mission began its work a bit later and continues to oversee churches in the region.[8]

7. The lone sewing machine in Legua 17, gift of Evita Perón, 1988

THE PENTECOSTAL MESSAGE

In my doctoral dissertation (Miller 1967:226ff.), I argued that established Christian mission ideology reflects the "highly institutionalized and secularized values" of the colonial nations that sponsor them; furthermore, such ideology "is generally incongruent with aboriginal belief systems inseparably connected to all of life's experiences." The fundamental thesis was that a society such as that of the Toba can only confront missionary teaching in terms of its own philosophical grasp of the ideas presented, and that it interprets and adapts those elements perceived as aiding in the resolution of problems conceptualized by the society's own members (see also Worsley 1968). In other words, indigenous people take an active role in the reinterpretation and incorporation of missionary teaching; they are not passive recipients who simply absorb missionary doctrine as presented to them. Furthermore, the notion of a Christian God was not new to the Toba, given the history of Jesuit and Franciscan efforts in the region; thus a vocabulary for Protestant missionary teaching was already in place.

Significantly, Pentecostalism represented the least secularized form of Christianity offered to the Eastern Toba, particularly the preinstitutionalized form of it they adopted. I explained its rapid and widespread success throughout the region in the 1950s and 1960s in terms of its compatibility with a traditional shamanic ideology that stressed direct encounter with spiritual powers for purposes of physical and emotional healing, as well as its arrival at a moment of crisis in Toba history when new leadership with a new ideology was in demand (Miller 1967, 1979).

The story of Pentecostalism's success can be told best by participants who were at the center of its active growth and expansion. The following accounts, taped during my missionary encounter with the Toba from 1959 to 1963, depict not only Toba recollections of initial mission actions, but also the *culto* rhetoric that intermingles traditional symbolic themes and logic with Christian ones reinterpreted by the individual speakers, who range from *culto* pastors to lay preachers to political community leaders.

First Testimony

Today I want to tell you about where I came from when I first accepted the Word, the Word of our God. When the Word first reached us, we heard it from Resistencia and I liked it very, very much. But it wasn't only that I liked the message, I had an affliction at that time. That was the reason I heard our Father's Word and accepted without delay, because I was in need. I had done everything possible to seek medical help that might heal me when the Word had not yet arrived. I searched long and hard for that in which to put my trust. I went everywhere among our people searching for a means to save my life, but I could not find it. I even came to submit myself to powerful *ltaxaÿaxaua* [Speaking Companions], because you must understand that at that time there were many of those powers which we called our defense, our pythonic magicians. Thus, when I was sick, I entrusted myself to no one but them because, as you know, they were our only hope. And the day arrived when I could not encounter what I needed, a means to save my life. When I was carried lying down to the one who was to heal me, he would only say that there was no cure for my illness.

It was then that the power arrived that can cure any illness. At once I told myself not to delay, because I had a sickness that had reached every part of my body. Therefore I left, I went then to Resistencia because I heard the name of Jesus Christ, the only Savior, the only Healer. I did not wait, despite the fact that my father forbade me to go. I escaped anyway because there was a reason why my elders opposed my going; they were shamanic healers (*pi'oxonaq*). Why, then, could they not heal me if they were healers?

Nevertheless, those men had power in which they trusted. For that reason I want to tell you about this, for all of these reasons I want you to know and understand, because then you will comprehend our old customs (*n'onataguec*), which certainly today we say were lies. Now we have entered the gospel and we must also evaluate and question whether it is absolutely true. Because that is how it is, my brothers.

When I escaped, my human father did not allow me to go where the people were congregating, but I paid no attention, I only proceeded on foot to Resistencia. However, I was very ill and for that reason my walk took a week and a half to arrive, because they took me slowly; I could not walk rapidly or at a normal pace. I also left early to escape from my father because he did not want me to go. But I paid no attention because I was very sick and I went together with my uncles who had already believed the Word.

It was the year 1940 when we went to Resistencia. We left La Pampa on foot, but we still arrived at Resistencia. When I arrived in Resistencia, there was a church service that night and the preacher was speaking, announcing and preaching in the name of Jesus Christ. That same night I submitted. I said, "Well, for this reason I have come, to accept the name of Jesus Christ." And that same night I was healed; I was given life that night. This is my story. The only thing I have done is continue on until the present time; I have survived until today.

Well, my brothers, I am telling you about my experience with the gospel because, my brothers, I want you my known brethren to think about [pay attention to] my experience. I am not ashamed nor afraid to recount my experience because for twenty years I have dedicated my efforts entirely to the Word, and even more now that we know well its just way. For that reason I get even more strength from the Word and I want my brothers not to leave the Word, which is why I am telling about my way, my knowledge of the gospel.

Because long ago when the gospel had not yet arrived, when the Word of our God had not yet arrived here, we had our customs which are called tribal customs, or our own ways of doing things. And those practices caused us to suffer, they ruined us; they caused us harm and disgrace, they did not bring us good, only evil. We were completely abandoned and lost because of our customs. That is why I find them disgusting, my brethren. I despise them because I now see myself as a true child of God. This is the cause that I now pursue, I am preaching the work of God. I know my brethren and I am searching among them, some days with tears, so that they might all become believers.

Now we have come to know the nature of the work, that it is no ordinary thing, that it is complete life, that it is medicine for the person with sickness inside because it gives life, it heals. This is the basis for what I have seen. Why, then, would I not pursue this work with diligence? Why would I not make every effort to enlist others in the work I am doing? There are days when I wish there were others who would commit themselves to the work in which we are engaged. When we engage ourselves together in the work, it will grow rapidly; peace will prevail and our work will expand. When we agree in our thinking, the work will not diminish, it will grow. And now we reach the final request and our work will be complete.[9]

I am saying this because the day will come when people will come here to the house of our brother where I am at this moment, and they can listen to my thoughts about our work and dedicate themselves diligently to it. I say this to all of you, my brethren, because I want all of our brothers to put on a good heart and good thoughts, although this is difficult when one has not yet surrendered one's self. But nothing is impossible with God; he is able to transform a person, and when he does, that person, like me, can speak about the work.

Yes, my brothers, we had our ancient customs, our practices. There were days when these customs had us congregated together under the control of pythonic magicians; we stood before shamans who cured; we united in the frog dance to the music of drums. During the night we would stumble over drunkards in the paths. The way of wine is to cause harm, the same for the drums and dance, the pythonic magicians. But now only one thing guides us, our gospel work. It is not superstition, it is not bad habits, it is not magic. It is completely the work of God, and the person who surrenders his life finds life and peace. You know that this is true. The one who learns this truth will have a great peace, because as the Word says, "If you know the truth, it shall make you free." I also wish to give my name, my name is Aurelio López.[10]

Aurelio López (photograph 8) was the first president of the independent Toba IEU, the one who traveled widely to spread its message and set up regional representatives throughout the Chaco region. His testimony describes the core of the *culto* message—faith healing versus shamanistic curing and peaceful relations with God and fellow human beings—that came to captivate every indigenous community. Church buildings were erected, pastors were authorized to preach, members were baptized, and services were held in every settlement in the region. Within twenty years the *culto* had spread to neighboring groups of Mocoví and Wichí as well, and even to Paraguay and the region of the upper Pilcomayo River. Community life centered around *culto* activity, even for those who failed to officially join the congregations. Few *culto* leaders drew the clear distinction Aurelio did between the *culto* message and traditional shamanism. The following account of a widely respected layman places the story of *culto* growth in broader historical perspective.

Second Testimony

I was born here at Quintilipi in the Indian reservation. My parents were from El Espinillo, but there was a big flood and my mother escaped with my father and came to La Reducción (the reservation) where I was born about 1917.

I remember my uncle Juan Burgo, my mother's brother, and also Chief Alberto Burgo's brother. These people were Dapicoshic, but they lived in La Reducción.[11] At

Photograph 8. Aurelio López and family circa 1960

that time there was an 'oiquiaxai [powerful spirit] named Julio Macha.' The police killed a hut full of people because they robbed and killed white people. My parents, especially mom, remember that very well. My father taught me not to rob or to fool around. So at that time when many people were killed, my Uncle Juan Burgo went to Buenos Aires with Chief Francisco Moreno from Las Palmas and they asked for a big parcel of land for the people. The Land Director went also. Juan Burgo was mixed with white ancestry. Moreno asked for Las Palmas, the Land Director asked for La Pampa del Indio, and Juan Burgo asked for El Espinillo. That must have been about 1914. Each one represented his people: Taguiñil'ec, people from the east, represented by Francisco Moreno and the Land Director, and Dapigueml'ec, northwesterners, represented by Juan Burgo. These three were the first chiefs to pacify the people. All of Burgo's people went with him to El Espinillo. Whenever there was danger, the people came south. I remember when we traveled between El Espinillo and La Reducción. We went with a lot of people. I remember passing a sawmill. At that time there were a lot of deer and wild pigs and we were hunting as we migrated south. Sáenz Peña was only a small town with a train station. There were no settlers in Tres Isletas or Castelli. There were only aborigines. There were guns and arrows, also.

When I was fifteen years old, we went to harvest in Sáenz Peña. It was my first time, even though Juan Burgo had already planted cotton. We were paid sixty cents for ten kilos. A shirt cost sixty cents and shoes cost twenty cents. We all went from El Espinillo to harvest cotton in order to buy clothing because there in El Espinillo we did not have any. At that time the people became migrant laborers because there was work here. Each year we went to harvest, and only my parents stayed to keep house. They planted corn, squash, and so forth, and hunted.

My parents taught me not to hunt without a license and to marry only one woman. They taught me to work and not to steal and not to drink, because one can lose a great deal, nor should I smoke because when I throw away the cigarette butt, someone could pick it up to do harm and kill me [sorcery]. My uncles also taught me in this manner. This is not gospel, but it is knowledge. One was not to get married unless he knew how to hunt, to ride a horse, and build a house. When one had learned all of this, then he could marry. The men married older, but the women were very young. First one had to talk with the girl's parents. Sometimes the parents were good and advised against marrying their daughter. One could live in either the house of the woman or the man. The parents talked among themselves to decide where the newlyweds would live. They also taught how one should treat a woman. My sister wanted to marry a Dapicoshic, but my father did not want her to because he was an outsider. I have had the same woman for twenty-seven years. I never had another.

When my father died, he taught me that I should get along with everyone. He was very good; he never taught me anything bad. My mother's father was very bad. He was a doqshil'ec [white man]; his name was Soxoÿaxauaic in Toba and Abram Díaz in Spanish. He talked rough. He lived among the Indians for seventeen years. In two years he understood our language completely, although his mother was half qomlashi [Toba]. Grandfather was very good, nevertheless; he called the people to work in the sugarcane. He got smallpox and died in Salta.

Now I will talk about the time of the gospel. In 1934 Juan Tomás Palmar [British Emmanuel Mission] asked permission to teach our people. First he asked Jesús Bachorí, but he did not agree. Then he asked Alberto Burgo, and he did not want him on his land but on our land; that is, on his brother's land. Our land was sandy. My brother said, "Of course, if he teaches the families." That was in 1934 and I was seventeen years old. They put up four buildings. One was a clinic, another a market, still another for prayer, and the remaining one was a house for himself. This brother attracted a lot of attention because it was the first time any of us had heard of the gospel. He invited people to come from far and wide: from Pozo la China, Tres Pozos, La Paloma, Palo Mar, Río Muerto, Paso Sosa, La Serena, La Confluencia, and everywhere. And people from all these places went to live there. There were many people. From Lavalle everyone went. In Tres Pozos, Jesús Bachorí remained and did not go because his father objected.

This man taught carpentry, school, church, and hospital. They made material things. He was there seven years and then went back to his country to get married. He announced that he was going back to visit his mother and he returned with a wife. When his father died, he took everything with him and did not return. Enrique Tuck did not baptize anyone, he only taught, gave seed and credit. Few people accepted, even though many went to the services. When Enrique left, Stephen came. He left and Valenciano came. Stephen sold Avila's things for 40,000 pesos. Few people were coming; they did not want the gospel.

When they were ready to sell out, a Toba arrived and went to advise the police. Lorenzo went and explained that the owner had ordered the demolition of the mission. Raúl Roldán ordered that the house not be destroyed. It was to be left alone. They went to the judge and made a law requiring that nobody touch the house. They left a fellow Toba in charge by the name of Lorenzo. It was the missionaries themselves who abandoned the mission, not the government.[12]

When the Pentecostals arrived, I felt like joining. After the missionaries left, the work came to a standstill; there were no services. Only when the Pentecostals came, they opened services again in another building, and later in Pozo la China.

It was Pedro Martínez who arrived to start the Pentecostal work in 1946. He worked with Marco Mazzucco.[13] Chief Martínez named Pancho Pellegrini pastor and Valentín Segundo assistant pastor. Many people became part of this work. But when Pancho died and no Pentecostal visitor came, the work died and remains dead to this day.

I got married in Tres Isletas during the harvest. My wife's family was also from El Espinillo. I went to my wife's parents' house in Río Muerto. My father-in-law gave me land to work, a plow, and oxen. He was Juan Fernández's grandfather. My father and my brother taught me farm work. Our fathers were good farmers, they learned from criollos. I continued working the farm and sold cotton to Roldán. The missionaries also gave seed, but they kept it for the dry weather.

For three years I prayed to God in order to be able to leave my place there in El Espinillo. It seems that God answered because during this year 1962 I became sick. The illness was very serious. It was pneumonia. When it came to me, I sent my wife out to harvest and I remained at home to take care of the old people. She did not want to leave me, but I insisted. I found a woman to take care of the old people. I wanted to get into the hospital, but they did not reach my number.[14] Finally I ran into a brother from Jehovah's Witness. He helped me very much through prayer. He respected me very much because he told me that medicines were poisonous and that God was going to heal me. In two weeks I felt better and was healed. I returned to where my brother was and sent to look for my wife because I was healed through prayer. When I was healed, I went to the services at Pampa Argentina, although I did not go before because I was ashamed. Juan Pablo's first wife was my first cousin. She asked me to stay with her, and I accepted. This is all I have to say. My name is Gregorio Díaz.

This account is particularly interesting in that it documents the nomadic movement of Toba families between the various Toba settlements during the speaker's lifetime. It also recounts a history of the El Espinillo Emmanuel Mission very much in keeping with that recorded in official documents. Díaz was an active layman who took an interest in *culto* concerns. Note his focus on personal healing and quick acceptance of the Pentecostal message, as opposed to that of the Emmanuel Mission. His distinction between knowledge taught by his parents and the gospel does not appear to involve the disjunction affirmed in the previous account.

The following recording documents the close link between shamanic themes and *culto* activity. The injection of traditional mythic themes into a testimony about one's personal faith is characteristic of *culto* messages I have heard over the years. This account is of particular interest since it is offered by a lay preacher who readily acknowledges his shamanic identity.

Third Testimony

I will give my testimony and everyone can hear it. I am completely changed. I am called Carlos Soxonaic. I am a shaman, also. I cure illnesses. Actually, I have quit practicing. Of whom am I prisoner? No mere human caught me, I am the catch only of Jesus Christ. I am content. I speak of my great joy today. I am with my brothers Emilio and Alberto.[15] I love my brothers very much. Now I am assisting them. I am giving my testimony. I am giving it, giving it totally. I am being pursued by all the problems that plague me, but I pay them no attention; my children all come to help me. I saw my sons die, but I continue to praise our Father God. Our life does not come from any other, only from God Himself. Jesus Christ stripped me of mundane things; he showed me the way that leads to Heaven. And I am only speaking of my gratitude now. Even until now I am being pursued and I am confronting what is called illness. But I don't know, my Father himself helps me. In this manner I know the help that I receive. I know very well the message of the Lord Jesus Christ. Well, the main point is that I am content with my brothers Emilio and Alberto; we continue hand-in-hand. These are my brothers. This is my only joy because I have already given myself over, but completely. Now I follow face-to-face with the Word of my Father. Well, that is all I have to say about my joy.

I was with my son when his illness arrived, but I did not understand it. The illness continues to dominate him as though it were natural. When his life is restored, I will comprehend better how much pity God has for my requests night after night. There are days when all day long I think about where I can go for help, but I always go to God. My son is sick and I do not know if he will be healed. Perhaps in these very days. I only have a deep peace within. That is the end of my message about my children.

• • •

The sorcerer kills in the following fashion. If there is a reason she gets angry, or perhaps does not have food to eat, then she says, "They are fooling with me." Then she says, "I will kill that person. He always brings things home to eat, but he offers me nothing. Therefore I will kill that man. The only thing I will do is single him out for death, because he has been staring at me for many days. He does not like me and I do not like him; therefore I am going to do it. I will grab my evil power, but first I will request illness from the one who gives it. Then I will kill him." That is all I have to say about it, brother.

What am I thinking about? Yes, that I am a *pi'oxonaq* [shaman]. There are days when I have pity on my brother. But when he does not care about me, I do not care about him. Then things happen in the following manner: if I do not like one when he does not offer me anything, perhaps his pants if I ask for them, if he does not give them to me, then I hate him. But my hatred is of the sort that will only kill him. Because there is no one equal to me. I am a *pi'oxonaq*. I am an assassin. At that point another shaman speaks up. He says, "You will not be able to kill this person when I get there. It is you I will kill. I am more powerful than you. You aren't worth anything. It is true that you have your earthly Companion Spirit, but I have a Companion Spirit from the Sky. I will kill you. I take pity on my brother and you are not going to kill him." Then I speak again, I say, "No, you will not kill me; when I kill the sick person, I will pay you." Well, then the friendly shaman gives in and he agrees to what the bad shaman said. That is all I have to say on that subject.

Well, there was a person that Salamanca cared for.[16] He loved that person. Then Salamanca said the following: "I am coming to you. I love you. I am going to give you your own power, but our power is located inside the water. We are going to be water beings. My name is Salamanca. No one can kill me. I, myself, am an assassin. I am giving my power to you. It is my power, my own power. However, if there is a sick person, cure him. But if the person healed does not pay you, return the sickness. Thus you will not cure him. He will surely die. I am handing over my work [responsibilities] to you."
Then the person who was loved said, "You, Salamanca, I agree that you are my master. I beg your forgiveness, but the person that I save [heal], I will save, but there will be no payment." But Salamanca responded, "No, I cannot permit that. The person that you save sometime in the future will take advantage of you because he does not know where he acquired his life. It is much better that you request something from the person you heal. If he has a horse, ask for it. Then you will have an animal to take care of. I tell you this because I love you. You are poor. You are a person. You wander about the countryside [hunting]. But I am Salamanca. I love you and I want you to have the things you need. If you do not demand payment, I will not be in agreement. Then I will kill you." Then the loved person said, "Well, then, I will do what you say, Salamanca. Thus, when I heal someone, I am going to ask for something, whether it be a shotgun or perhaps a horse. Only if I am able to cure him, then I will request something. But if the person does not get healed, then I will not ask anything of him. The only thing I request is that you give me your true power. Then it will be your own power. In that way I will not be responsible." Then Salamanca responded, "No, have no fear, I really love you." That is the end of that tale.

• • •

Well, I am the North Wind. I go around looking for sick people. Because the sick person, when he has whatever infirmity inside, I rush in to help him die. I am the North Wind. I am visible. I am evil. I am bad. I do not love anyone. It is true that I am from the Sky, but I am different because I bring death. He who is always well continues to be well; he is my significant brother. He who is sick is not my brother and I only hurry to burn him.

Well, now the wind has turned around. Yes, well, now I am South Wind. I have a master. I am son of the South Wind and I am also capable of causing harm. If I find a sick person who is certainly going to die, then when I arrive I raise him up [heal him], because I bring the cold. I am Wind. I am son of the South Wind. And when I encounter a sick person, I make him rise because my power is great. I have mercy on the person who is healthy. I care for the person who cares for me. The only thing I give him is life. Thus, when I blow on his body, he rises up. I have great confidence wherever I go, because I chase away the North Wind; I carry him along. That is the end of the story.

What next? When this infirmity arrives, when it comes to you, you get sick. When you love me, then I do the following. I touch the part where you are in pain. When I find the illness, I say to you, "Listen to my breath that I am blowing down on you. I am blowing my breath, but you must listen. When you feel my breath, answer; you must respond to me. Well, I already blew my breath because I am touching the part that hurts. I have found what is causing you pain. It is in your chest. I blow down my breath. Tell me when you feel it. How are you feeling?" The sick person responds, "Yes, I feel your breath, my brother." Soxonaic says, "Alright then, I am happy. Now I am going to place my hand over the spot and you are going to get up. I will bite the illness and suck it out. Afterward, I will show it to you. OK, there it is, I show it to you." The sick one asks, "Where?" Soxonaic replies, "Is this what was making you scream?" The sick person says, "Yes, brother, that is what was giving me tremendous pain. What is this that gave me so much pain?" Soxonaic says, "Well, it is your blood. This is the only thing that was causing your pain. Therefore you can now go. Go home because you are well. Tell the people that your life came from me. That is the basis for your salvation." That is all.

I and this sick person, we ask you, Lord Jesus, to help us. You are here among us. We pray for this sick person. But this our brother who leads his brethren, our leader, we help him. He only places his hand on the spot that pains. And when the sick person speaks, he says, "I feel that my sickness has disappeared, because I heard your prayer." Then the sickness leaves, it goes slowly away. The hand of our Father God has tremendous power. Because our Father God, his name may appear to be a plaything, but when we feel something, then we call out his name. Our Father says the following: "My son, if you have something inside you and you need me, then call on me. Then the sick person is saved. One can be healed only through my name, because my name is not a plaything." Then the sick person speaks after hearing our prayer. We have a real fight on our hands. We are calling upon the Father of us all who is in the heavens, whose name is God. His son is named Christ. He, himself, is our master. He answers our clamoring prayers every day. You, sick person, speak when you hear the words we speak. They are not our words, they are from our Father who is called God. Speak when you are genuinely healed, then get up. The sick responds, "I am getting up, I am saved. I who am sick, I heard the messages of our Lord Jesus, the

Son of Man, the son of the one called God. Now I am content, I stand up, I am saved. You yourselves can see my salvation. Now I hear my illness going slowly away. My illness is giving me advice, saying, 'I am leaving you because the Word of your Father God arrived.' Therefore, I am content. I am the sick person who has risen up. That is the end of my infirmity. Goodbye. The illness cannot return because I have already received the prayer. The only thing I have is tremendous joy." That is how it is.

Well, I will speak again, but I am not thinking alone. I cannot remember some of these things, but my brother makes me remember; I am here with Emilio, Toqos. And he is making me speak because I know well the ways of our old-timer Pedro Martínez. Well, he went south, he went to Perón. He conversed with Perón, and Perón said, "Alright, Martínez, return, but take along good things, take the Word of our Father God so that when you arrive you can distribute it. You must not hide so that you are available on the day when things are given out. Because we do not know about our lives. Perhaps they will stop giving out things, but you have a brother who remembers your trip and he will remember to provide things for you."[17]

Well, our brother Pedro Martínez arrived at the church of our brother Tomás Palmer and asked for his blessing. "Give me work," he said. Tomás Palmer said, "It would be better for you to follow the gospel that is good so that when your brothers are gathered together, you will not grab a bottle of wine in your hand, only the Word of our Father you will grab. Because I know that you, Pedro Martínez, are a drinker. And now, you who do not pretend to follow the Word of our Father, who then will be your helper? It will be the person who is called Christ. This same person will save you. Afterward, you will demonstrate the work of our Father God."

Our brother Pedro Martínez said, "I will do it. Truly I will do it, because this will represent my complete change, in order that my sons will also change, so that they will know where to find their peace and their life. But when I do this, if my children are against it, then I will be the same to them. It is better for them to be separated out, standing before the Word of our God, standing before the work of our Lord Jesus. And I will carry around the message, but not only this. I have asked for a place in La Pampa. I am going to La Pampa. When I arrive, I will build a house. Then I will unite my sons who love the Word of God, and to those signaled out I will distribute our blessings. I am content because I know this. And now I am very happy that you showed me this way. Thus, when I arrive to where I am going, then I will go among the young people advising them about the Word of our God. Yes, there where I am going I will do it. I will do it. I will reveal the truth. And not only will I reveal it, I will make available this land so that they might cultivate; then no one will ever be at fault. I am completely overjoyed. You, Tomás Palmer, have shown me the Word of our Father God. I am called Pedro Martínez. My name is Qachiuñi." That is all I am able to say.

The intermingling of shamanic ideology and the gospel of healing is clearly portrayed in these recordings, but especially in the latter one.[18] The theme of the power of God and his Son Christ (others stress the Holy Spirit) to heal rather than kill is the dominant one emphasized in *culto* preaching. The nature of this power is comparable to that of Salamanca, the North

Wind and South Wind, or any other "Speaking Companion" (*ltaxaÿaxaua*) that empowers a shaman, but it is even more powerful and only heals; it never causes harm. In this way, the former sources of ambiguous power are contrasted with those of the gospel, which, theoretically, cures with no demand for payment.

The matter of payment has been and continues to be a sensitive point in Toba ideology. The shaman who does not extract payment always runs the risk of revenge from an empowering spirit that demands it. While this would appear to be a good excuse for charging the patient, the social demand for sharing quickly dissipated any serious collection of goods.

Any number of Toba pastors face the same dilemma when they make demands on the congregations they serve. The appropriation of *culto* offerings continues to be a dilemma for pastors, much as the demand for goods was for the traditional shaman. Aurelio López himself made demands for food and lodging that were sometimes resented by the people he served on his travels throughout the eastern Chaco. When his voice was silenced by a stroke, many said that it was shamanic revenge for his haughty demands. More than one shaman warned me against identifying with him too closely during our years with the Mennonite Mission.

The following testimony of Juan Acosta (photograph 9), a practicing Toba pastor in the eastern part of La Reducción during the early 1960s, depicts further the syncretic nature of traditional Toba mythology and *culto* practice. I originally entitled the transcription of this recording "Juan Acosta's Visions."

Fourth Testimony

A long time ago I received a vision that came from the sky. I saw three colors: blue, red, and yellow. Then I saw a person who spoke to me and said, "I give you power to heal the sick, and whoever comes for help you must heal." He gave me a song in order to cure, and one should give what he receives. My Companion Spirit did not give me medicine, only the song. He said the power came from God. Well, I healed many sick people. But I never asked for anything in return, I only received what they gave me voluntarily.

Subsequently, as there were many shamans, envy developed among the others because I had healed many sick people. Then another vision came to me through my Companion Spirit. In the vision I was told that other shamans wanted to kill me because I healed many people and the sick no longer went to them for curing because they charged for their services.

Subsequently I had another vision. A "man" descended from the sky and called the other shamans together. He told them to quit causing me trouble and to love me and get along with me. After that, all those who wanted to be great came to an end. They died.

When I was converted, I also had a vision. I saw a person who talked to me. He said, "Look, my son, do not look any longer at the other things around you, but you must always look to me." This vision came in the Pampa Aguará Mission. There I

9. Juan Acosta circa 1962

must always look to me." This vision came in the Pampa Aguará Mission. There I was baptized [according to mission records, on May 25, 1955].

Some two months later I had a pain in my heart and my heart beat heavily for about four days. I had a vision about this pain. There was a man who was jealous of my daughter. This handsome man asked, "Why do you eat and drink what this one gives you which is not yours?" The other powerful Companion said, "Go away, you do not have anything to do with him anymore," and the former one never came to me again. It was that vision which taught me that one should look only above and not to this earth.

Subsequently I had another vision. A black person was walking from the south toward the north in the sky. A voice said, "I, too, can do my work." The person was walking in the sky. The last vision I saw was men with wings in the sky. They spoke and said, "All that listen we will make understand." They took out swords and punished many people.

In another vision I saw a church and beautiful corn. Suddenly an owner came out and asked me, "Who gave you permission to come here? You must return." He took out a revolver and made me turn back. After returning back I was not satisfied because I asked myself how a son of God could not go where he had to go, to the brethren. I returned and the man came out angry and asked why I had returned. I told him that I am a son of God and that I must go to my people, and he returned to the house without saying anything. This and many other visions I had.[19]

My father was a shaman, but he did not teach me the secret. They say there are those who give virtue and power to their sons. I did not suck out objects, only blood and pus. I distrust those who say they suck out wood, bone, or whatever. Power [napinshic] comes by means of a vision.

In 1944 I became tremendously ill. All of a sudden an older man came to me, an old man; he pointed out to me two women and asked me if I knew them. He said their names, and I said that I did. He said, "They want to kill you." I wanted to go with him to find the object of mine they had which they were using to cause me harm. He said, "No, I will go to look for it myself." From that moment I was completely healed.

Acosta was pastor of an active *culto* in the national reservation southeast of Napalpí. Note the lack of tension or incompatibility between the symbolic world of shamanism and that of his current experience in the *culto*.

Since Acosta lived in the area of La Matanza (The Killing), where the famous "episode" of 1924 occurred in which many Toba were killed by provincial police (described in my dissertation and subsequently [Miller 1967, 1979, 1995], a significant event that may have helped spark the *culto* movement), he often spoke about it during our interactions in the early 1960s. On one occasion, he recorded the following text that provides an additional perspective on the topic of payment to leaders who heal.

We were in the house of Macha' [leader in command of the people congregated at Napalpí in 1924] for a week or so, but my father had a vision that it would turn out badly, so we escaped secretly by day in order that he would not be angry. From there we went to Machagai, which at that time was the old town. The people danced every night and in the daytime as well.

The people lost confidence after they saw the bullets killing. There was a big loss of confidence. Just like today if a preacher announces that he has power but does not keep his promise. The leaders had announced that a "man" came out from the earth telling our people to kill whites. This "man" was a liar. I also managed to greet the one from under the earth; he had a soft, limp hand. It was white. There was a line formed in order to greet him. It was in a house, a long house made of grass. We came close to the house and we greeted him. He was inside and we were outside.

Many people say that a preacher should not work in material things. The idea came from the early preachers who announced that the people should not work because the blessing will come if they have faith. I teach my people to work in the fields and to earn in order to build our church. We offer salvation and strength, but we ourselves do not have it if we wait for it to come externally.

In my dissertation and elsewhere (especially Miller 1971), I point out that chiefs and/or shamans also played a key role in the formation and character of local *culto* activity. The settlement at Legua 15, where the Aguará Mission had established a church, was led by Chief Ernesto Petizo. Mission records suggest that he gave many an early missionary a hard time. By the time of our arrival in 1959, however, his relationship with the church had taken on a different flavor. The following recording, made on December 19, 1959, demonstrates the extent to which *culto* rhetoric came to constitute an essential component of his own experience.

Fifth Testimony

Peace, brothers, I am very happy to be with you here today. But we continue to be in need, all of us everywhere. Today we are standing in the good way, which is the reason that people are seeking out that which is good. The good is difficult to obtain, but God already knows us. Therefore, the only thing that we continue to request is the one called the Holy Spirit, who is capable of penetrating every person. I am carrying my gratitude, my thankfulness, and the gratitude of us all. My gratitude reaches to everyone. What more is there to do, because gratitude has been expressed on earth? The Son of God already looked upon us, and he is the only one who can help us. He came to us of his own accord because he sees that we are in need. He sees our need for the good way. We are thankful today that we are standing here where we are. What we need no one can supply except God, because he is the one who provides that which we are needing.

Yes, I am extremely grateful to be here with Augusto Soria, Cavito Leiva, Juan Alegre, Lorenzo Soria, and my other nephews.[20] I have my name, my name is Ernesto Petizo, and my name is Loqten. But my thoughts only come from God, because they are not my own. Thus what I am saying today comes from him who has asked me to help with the Lord's work. I will be very grateful when our Father God truly causes to increase that which we call understanding, because while I have quite a bit of insight, it is necessary for it to grow. That is why I love the Word because what is required for my well-being has already been brought here. The truth is that here where we are on the earth the Lord Jesus has been for quite some time, because he left his blood here on this earth when he saw our great need, and he left with us what is called the Holy Spirit. Brethren, we are always grateful to our brother Emilio with whom we are gathered once again today. He is already our brother and thus he has a name; the name they gave him is Toqos.

Furthermore, he truly was sent out by our Father. Brother Albert already has a name, but you all know that his name is Llaanoxochi. We are highly grateful to our brothers with whom we are always together, but it is God who is the only one who helps us. Well, they have patience with us in our need, because we are always in need. You my brethren know very well that our need is obvious, but even greater is our need for that which is not seen. We are in need of the name of the Holy Spirit. You my brothers from all over, all of you are content; there is contentment, brethren. As the Apostle James says in verse two of Chapter 1, James says this, my brothers: "My brethren, whenever you have to face trials of many kinds, count yourselves supremely happy in the knowledge that such testing of your faith breeds fortitude." We already know, my brothers, the various sufferings that there are in this world, but we also know this verse. Therefore we are all grateful, we are happy to be here. Thus we will do, indeed we will demonstrate, good deeds, and they will be completely known. How could I say that we do not know? It is certainly true that we know the power of God.

There is power, there is power, there is power, Lord; there is, there is, Lord. Glory be to Jesus. There is, my Father God. You are my Father God, my Father God, you have mercy on me, help me because I do not know anything. You, my Father God, I place before you that which I am in need of today. You know that I do not know anything. You also know my need, that I am full of need, that I am very much in need of good things and for that reason I call upon you.[21] But the main point is that you have compassion on me because I always put before you my need. It is true that there are always those things that are already here, that you make me stand in your blessings. How, then, can I say that I am in misery since I already have the mercy, the richness of your dear name? Oh Father, the one I seek to emulate, I am crying out always about my love of your name which is always the same, that you might cause to arrive in my heart its trembling so that my brothers might hear of the good way that we are following.

What is remarkable about this recording is the fact that it sounds more like missionary rhetoric than the sermons of most *culto* leaders. Yet Petizo's role was strictly that of political leader in Legua 15, and he seldom if ever appeared in the *culto* on our visits there. What he meant by need is not spelled out in the recording, but it is clear from other conversations that he was referring to the state of physical and intellectual poverty in which he and his people found themselves vis-à-vis both missionaries and the broader Argentine society.

THE CONTEMPORARY SCENE

During the formative years of La Iglesia Evangélica Unida in the 1950s and 1960s, social tensions within and between communities tended to center around competition for clientele involving *culto* leaders and traditional shamans. Until that time, the isolated communal settlements had little, if any, official dealings with one another, other than the interactions of family members visiting back and forth. With the formation of the IEU, however, an annual assembly of the religious body came to be held where a president and regional representatives were selected or reconfirmed. It was at this juncture that a more formal linkage of isolated social units began to take shape. Preachers and singing groups began to travel around the region to participate in local *cultos*, with the result that communication between settlements became both more common and more focused. Along with *culto* rhetoric, discussions and debates about job opportunities, land rights, state policies and actions, competition for votes among national parties, and other issues came to involve a broader social scale than had been the case perhaps at any time in Toba history.

These actions must be situated within the broader national context of post-Perón politics, in which a growing number of political parties sought to gain popular support. In the Chaco, this process included campaigns in local Toba communities with the aim of capturing indigenous votes. The competition for votes involved promises of better things to come (the civilization process at work), as well as tangible rewards in the here and now. As was the case elsewhere, the immediate rewards were mostly a disappointment, and the promises were largely ephemeral. Meanwhile, families split over party loyalty, and communities competed for the limited goods available. The significant point from the perspective of this chapter is that national political competition for indigenous votes fostered broader social consciousness across communal boundaries, often creating tensions that had not existed previously.

Meanwhile, competition for the hearts and lives of the Toba also became a growing concern among international and national nongovernmental organizations. Whereas the Mennonite Mission to the IEU restricted financial support to missionary families, providing no direct assistance to Toba preachers or congregations other than transportation in mission jeeps or the sharing of food and blankets while traveling, other NGOs arrived in the Chaco during the 1970s and 1980s with more direct material assistance. Some of these were based in Europe, such as OXFAM, Bread for the World, and the Swedish mission Fundación del Buen Pastor; others were nationally based, such as the Protestant projects generated by the United Board of Missions (JUM), the Catholic actions sponsored by the Institute of Popular Culture (INCUPO), or the more strictly developmental efforts of the National Institute of Social Development (INDES). The Inter-American Foundation also provided support for rural development in several Toba and Mocoví settlements. These and other agencies have also stimulated broader self-awareness, directly or inadvertently, as they energize regional actions planned and focused on specific ethnic groups such as the Toba.

The reorganization of the Formosa and Chaco state Agencies for Indian Affairs into Institutes with elected indigenous leadership in 1984 and 1988, respectively, further expanded regional self-awareness as the Toba, Mocoví, Wichí and Pilagá became obligated to compete for representation by selecting individuals to represent them in these bodies. Since the candidates are compelled to campaign regionally for support, they acquire obligations to communities far from their home communities that sometimes conflict with local interests. In this process, communal groups compete for limited resources, and individuals take on responsibilities for much larger social units than were characteristic of traditional leadership, even in times of war when local bands congregated into larger units for more effective action.[22]

Bilingual school programs designed by the state to prepare indigenous students to teach school in their native languages also attract young people from distant provincial communities and distinct cultural identities into centers where ethnic awareness becomes intensified around common curricular concerns aimed at fostering appreciation for distinct cultural heritages. Here young Toba not only are made conscious of their own cultural traditions vis-à-vis those of other indigenous young people with different languages with whom they had no previous relationship, but also come to recognize identity with these former enemies vis-à-vis a national white society with its own traditions and history, of which they are also somehow a part. My own impression in 1997 was that in these schools, tomorrow's indigenous leaders are developing self-awareness on a scale unimagined previously.

CONCLUDING OBSERVATIONS

The subtitle of this chapter describes the expansion of Toba self-consciousness and determination in vitalistic terms. The idea suggests vivification, bringing to life a positive sense of peoplehood at a time when affirmative notions of identity were in sore demand. This was, in essence, the argument of my dissertation. I imagined the *culto* movement in positive terms as a means of generating a sense of cohesion and brotherhood in the face of social and economic deprivation imposed externally by the nation-state, and as a place where individuals could take charge of their lives in the full confidence that Toba beliefs and actions need not look to white society for verification.

I would argue, in retrospect, that the *culto* has provided a haven where the Toba language and tradition have been valued, and where Toba concerns on a variety of topics can be expressed. There has also been strength in numbers in that the demand for justice—for land, health care, jobs, and education—is made with greater passion and conviction, given the greater awareness of the number of people involved.

However, the initial aim to establish an independent united evangelical church where estranged people could unite in common cause has proven to be as ephemeral as the proverbial politician's promises. Competition among *culto* leaders for financial support from one or more of the many governmental agencies and NGOs, as well as for power and prestige, has generated divisions and accusations that have pitted region against region and brother against brother. At the time of this writing, two separate pastors claim to be president of the IEU, the Formosa Province has threatened to break away to form its own religious organization, and the Chaco provincial Institute of Chaco Aborigines (IDACH) has been closed down while indigenous leaders have been put in jail, charged with fraud. One promising young church leader who was asked to run for an institute position last year became so disgusted with the entire operation that he withdrew with the comment "I can no longer participate in this process, since one is obliged to tell lies in order to get elected."

The leadership state of affairs has become so serious that many claim, "There are no credible leaders today, neither shamans, pastors, nor politicians."[23] This credibility problem comes, unfortunately, at a time when the Toba face economic hard times as Argentina moves to participate more actively in the global economy by selling off its national resources to international business interests. Lack of resources in rural Chaco settlements drives increasing numbers of Toba to urban areas, where the jobless rates are already well over 20 percent. But this is subject matter for a different chapter.

NOTES

1. See Balmori (1957:24–25), Pelleschi (1886), and Lafone Quevedo (1893:12), among others, for a discussion of the Guaraní origin of the term "Toba" with its reference to "face," or possibly "across" (the river). Orbigny (1837) clearly noted the distinction between Eastern and Western Toba, but it was largely ignored by well-known twentieth-century researchers, such as Alfred Métraux (1946) and Rafael Karsten (1932).

2. In Father Gabril Patiño's diary entry of November 29, 1721, four persons approach the Patiño party with the statement "We are Tobas and we bring our leader" (Patiño 1833, in Arenales, op. cit., p. 26).

3. My initial field experience was with the Mennonite Board of Missions, Elkhart, Indiana, from 1959 to 1963; I returned for further research as an anthropologist in 1966, 1972, 1979, 1988, and (briefly) 1997. See Miller (1995) for an account of these distinct encounters with the Eastern Toba.

4. The voices selected here were recorded primarily during our initial stay in the Chaco when Toba leaders who visited our house in Sáenz Peña would ask to speak on the tape recorder with a message for fellow Toba visitors who might arrive. A number of these tapes have yet to be transcribed.

5. For a description of the Emmanuel Mission, see Sockett (1966).

6. The Mennonites visited the Emmanuel Mission in El Espinillo and modeled theirs after it. Several Toba families joined the Aguará Mission, as did a missionary

when the Espinillo Mission was closed. See Shank (1951) for an account of the Mennonite mission to the Toba.

7. See William Reyburn's report (1954) to the Mennonite Board of Missions at Elkhart, Indiana.

8. For a broader discussion of initial Protestant missions to the Chaco, see Miller 1967:98–107, reproduced in 1979:81–91 and 1980:67–77. See Wright (1990) for a description of a Foursquare Gospel *culto*.

9. Here I assume that López is referring to the authorization of the IEU by the Ministry of *Cultos* in Buenos Aires.

10. I recorded this message in 1960 on one of Aurelio's visits to our home in Sáenz Peña, a time when my wife and I traveled widely in the Chaco visiting Toba settlements where Aurelio preached and authorized local church leadership. He was the one who sparked the growth and extension of the *culto* movement, with the assistance of ex-Aguará Mennonite missionaries Albert and Lois Buckwalter, with whom my wife and I worked from 1959 to 1963.

11. Dapicoshic (Honey People) constitutes one of the regional kin categories mentioned earlier. They occupied the region northwest of Castelli (see map 9) where *dapic*, a wild honey stored underground, was commonly found.

12. This is an interesting perception, since the Emmanuel missionaries all blame the mission's demise on opposition from a local priest who convinced provincial officials to have them removed.

13. Marco Mazzucco was head of the Church of God Pentecostal in Buenos Aires at the time.

14. People arriving at the hospital in Castelli were given a number to wait in line for attention. The author does not mention that prior to the establishment of a mission hospital there a decade later, Indians found it difficult to get examined when there were whites in line.

15. The Toba called me Emilio or my Toba name Toqos. Alberto was the missionary colleague who formerly had worked with the Aguará Mission.

16. Salamanca is a spirit of the underworld in criollo mythology, at some point in colonial history incorporated into Toba cosmography. Although this is not stated overtly, I understood that the speaker was referring to his own experience here.

17. As we have seen in the previous testimony, it was not Perón but the Pentecostal pastor Marco Mazzucco who authorized Martínez to "distribute the Word." The notion of "cargo" to be distributed by the nation-state is a widespread theme among the Toba to this day.

18. For discussions of Toba shamanism, see Miller 1967, 1975, 1979; Cordeu 1969–70; and Wright 1992, 1997.

19. Acosta also had a vision the night before we arrived. He saw Bailón Domingo and me, along with many other visitors. Thus he was not surprised when we arrived.

20. All were shamanic and political leaders from the Miraflores area.

21. Given early missionary complaints about Petizo's haughty arrogance and his lack of interest in the *culto* at the time of this recording, these words came as a shock!

22. See Bray (1989) for a brief overview of the formation and goals of the provincial Institutes.

23. These comments were reported by Willis Horst, a Mennonite missionary located in Formosa City.

REFERENCES

Balmori, C. Hernando. 1957. Notas de un viaje a los Tobas. *Revista de la Universidad Nacional de La Plata* 2:23–36.

Bray, David. 1989. Indian Institutes in Argentina: From Paternalism to Autonomy. *Cultural Survival Quarterly* 13(3): 68–70.

Cordeu, Edgardo. 1969–70. Aproximación al horizonte mítico de los Tobas. *Runa* (Buenos Aires) 12(1–2):67–176.

Karsten, Rafael. 1932. *Indian Tribes of the Argentine and Bolivian Chaco*. Helsinki: Akademische Buchhandlung.

Lafone Quevedo, Samuel A. 1893–99. *Arte de la lengua Toba por el Padre Alonso Bárcena*. La Plata: Museo de La Plata.

Métraux, Alfred. 1946. Indians of the Chaco. In *Handbook of South American Indians*, ed. J. Steward, 1:197–370. Washington, D.C.: Smithsonian Institution, Bureau of American Ethnology.

Miller, Elmer S. 1967. Pentecostalism among the Argentine Toba. Ph.D. diss., University of Pittsburgh.

———. 1971. The Argentine Toba Evangelical Religious Service. *Ethnology* 10(2): 149–159.

———. 1975. Shamans, Power Symbols, and Change in Argentine Toba Culture. *American Ethnologist* 2(3): 477–496.

———. 1979. *Los Tobas Argentinos: Armonía y disonancia en una sociedad*. Mexico City: Siglo XXI.

———. 1980. *Harmony and Dissonance in Argentine Toba Society*. New Haven, Conn.: Human Relations Area Files, HRAFlex No. SI12–001.

———. 1995. *Nurturing Doubt: From Mennonite Missionary to Anthropologist in the Argentine Chaco*. Urbana: University of Illinois Press.

Orbigny, Alcide d'. 1837. *Voyage dans l'Amérique Méridionale (le Brésil, la République Orientale de l'Uruguay, la République Argentine, la République du Chili, la République de Bolivia, la République du Perou) exécuté pendant les années 1826–1833*. Vol. 2. Paris: Levrault.

Patiño, Gabril. 1833 [1721]. Diario del Padre Patiño. In *Noticias históricas y descriptivas sobre el Gran País del Chaco y Río Bermejo*, ed. J. Arenales, 15–28. Buenos Aires: Hallet y Cía.

Pelleschi, Giovanni. 1881. *Otto mesi nel Gran Ciacco: Viaggio lungo il fiume Vermiglio, (Río Bermejo) Mendoza, y Tucumán*. Firenze: Arte. Translated into English in 1886 as *Eight Months on the Gran Chaco of the Argentine Republic*. London: Sampson Low and Co.

Reyburn, William. 1954. *The Toba Indians of the Argentine Chaco: An Interpretive Report*. Elkhart, Ind.: Mennonite Board of Missions.

Shank, J. W. 1951. *We Enter the Chaco Indian Work*. Elkhart, Ind.: Mennonite Board of Missions.

Sockett, B. 1966. *A Stone Is Cast*. Birkenhead, Cheshire: Wrights'.

Worsley, Peter. 1968. *The Trumpet Shall Sound: A Study of "Cargo" Cults in Melanesia*. New York: Schocken Books, second augmented edition.

Wright, Pablo. 1990. Crisis, enfermedad, y poder en la Iglesia Cuadrangular Toba. *Cristianismo y Sociedad* 28(3):15–37.

———. 1992. Dream, Shamanism, and Power among the Toba of Formosa province, Argentina. In *Portals of Power: Shamanism in South America*, ed. E. Jean Matteson Langdon and Gerhard Baer, 149–172. Albuquerque: University of New Mexico Press.

———. 1997. "Being-in-the-Dream": Postcolonial Explorations in Toba Ontology. 2 vols. Ph.D. diss., Temple University.

7

※ ※ ——— ※ ※

Histories of Buenos Aires

Pablo G. Wright

This chapter focuses on the experience of Toba migrants in Buenos Aires.[1] Urban migrations within the Chaco region began in the 1950s when aborigines moved near towns,[2] shaping the so-called Toba barrios (Toba neighborhoods) in their peripheries.[3] Later, the circuit also widened to include other major cities outside the region.

While the Chaco was traditionally a rich and somehow "closed" ethnographic area, since the late 1950s it seems to have "expanded" its confines to include distant places, such as Rosario (Santa Fe Province) and Buenos Aires.[4] Indeed, many *qom* (Toba) migrated from their homeland, principally because of lack of work, transforming radically the ethnographic profile of the new places.[5] It was as if the Chaco established outlying spots of culture that implied a challenge for an anthropology that always conducted research in the far Chaco region. The new context raised questions about this notion. For example, could the *qom* remain themselves if they were away from their territory? Would they be able to maintain their identity surrounded by whites? What could be expected of this sociocultural encounter in an urban context? Would they maintain links with their homeland?

To partially answer and critique these questions,[6] this chapter explores the dimensions of life in Buenos Aires experienced by Valentín Moreno, a *qoml'ek* (Toba male) who moved there from Las Palmas (Chaco) in 1954. He is sixty-seven years old. His wife María died in 1993, leaving him with five children. The histories of Valentín's life in Buenos Aires (see map 10) are part of a general background he shared with me during multiple conversations undertaken since 1980. I met him during a seminar in linguistics at the University of Buenos Aires. Since then, we have developed a true friendship and mutual respect that have far exceeded the scientific project of learning Toba language and culture.

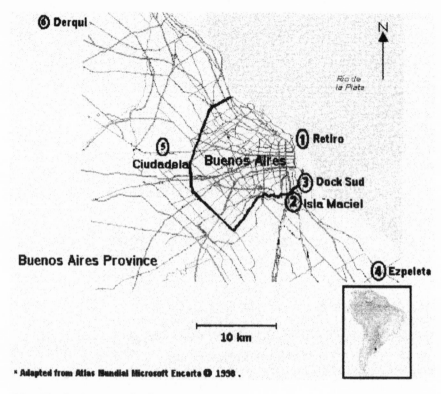

Map 10. Settlements of Valentín Moreno

These histories synthesize some of Valentín's major steps in Buenos Aires, with its ups and downs, joy and sorrow, revelation and loneliness, certainty and doubt. The idea is to show his perspective about different instances that cover our Western categories of everyday life, the sacred and the profane, labor, dreaming, and the dialectic of Indianness, identity, and politics.

From material recorded in formal and informal interviews in his home and at my own in suburban Buenos Aires, I selected a collection of vignettes that illustrate the power of a personal hermeneutic informed by a native cultural tradition.[7] Indeed, what Valentín calls *qom lataGak* (Toba way of life) is omnipresent in his accounts about both Chaco and Buenos Aires. Although he is installed in Buenos Aires, he maintains an "Indian thought" that expects to share with everybody, friends and strangers, *qom* and *doqshi* (whites). This is so because for him deep links bridge *qom lataGak* with *doqshi lataGak*, intermingled in Toba lore and biblical teachings.

Ultimately, I intend to show also that through individual experiences it is possible to trace the collective forces of society and history. In this case, Valentín's practice and recollections are a key field of encounter between subjectivity and structure within a given time and space. Histories in Buenos Aires narrate aspects of cultural life borne by an individual who struggles to be himself in spite of the urban odyssey of work, distance, and change.

NAME

Valentín's father, Francisco Moreno, was a major *cacique* (chief) of the Chaco Toba from 1910 to 1940 and worked in the Las Palmas sugar mill as *mayordomo* (manager).[8] His figure was well known across the region and also in the centers of power. Once he traveled to Buenos Aires to meet President Hipólito Yrigoyen. At that time, he also visited the Buenos Aires Zoo. Back in the Chaco, his baby son Valentín cried endlessly; nobody knew what happened to him. Ultimately, a *pi'ioGonaq* (shaman) arrived and found that an animal seen by Francisco in the zoo had "infected" (*nawoGa*) Valentín.[9] Indeed, because he had a baby, Francisco had to behave carefully; many situations could produce *nawoGa* in this context. To heal *nawoGa*, a negotiation was needed between the animal's spirit and the shaman. In this case, the former was satisfied by bestowing a new name on the baby.[10] Thus he received the name *onaGantak* and recovered quickly. Almost all Toba have both Toba and Spanish names. Valentín does not know what his Toba name means, but he regards it as an innermost part of his being.

ORIGINAL CONFLICT

After the death of *cacique* Moreno in 1940, his family lost everything. For that reason, Valentín and his brothers and sisters had to work for wages, either in the Las Palmas mill or on nearby farms in agriculture-related activities. From childhood, Valentín skillfully performed these tasks; he liked to ride horses all day long.

When Valentín was asked about the reason for going to Buenos Aires in the first place, he would associate it directly to problems with work. In late 1954 he was harvesting sugarcane in Las Palmas. After a week of hard work, he became angry at a foreman who refused to give him a wagon to load the harvest. It was a cold and rainy Sunday, and since Valentín felt sick from a chest pain, he went to the hospital. Though X rays did not show any injury, he was tired of being mistreated by his bosses; consequently, he decided to quit and try his luck in faraway Buenos Aires. In Las Palmas he felt helpless and without rights; maybe in the nation's capital he would find better and more adequate *trabajo* (work). *Trabajo* is a key term in Valentín's whole endeavor, as it is for many *qom* who ventured to the "rich" South.

IMAGES OF BUENOS AIRES

Valentín moved to Buenos Aires for "reasons of work." He had little knowledge beforehand of the city other than a few comments by *qom* who had traveled there. In this regard, he recalled one whom he asked how it was: "Well, it's very far and it seems pretty nice, but it's quite dangerous; you find good and bad people as well," the other replied. His words remained fresh in Valentín's memory, and after the wagon incident he considered that it was time for a change. His decision matched his itinerant wishes at the time "to stroll for its own sake," as he used to do throughout the Chaco province visiting relatives and trying different kinds of jobs. He was twenty-three years old.

FIRST TRIP

As usual in *qom* migrations within the Chaco region, Valentín wanted to have addresses of *qom* living in Buenos Aires, an essential link of an extended and very fluid social network. Distance and danger were not enough to stop him. Ultimately, he "got courage" to travel after receiving directions to find some Formosan people installed in Isla Maciel, a place south of the city in Buenos Aires Province.

In every sense, Buenos Aires differed from the Chaco. Valentín was not scared at all; however, his estrangement displayed the path of his interpretive framework. Isla Maciel was a poor neighborhood of the kind known in Argentina as *villa miseria* (slum). Valentín's earliest perceptions depict it dramatically: "We were all very crowded, completely crowded." The lack of an open space to look at annoyed him, as well as the scant room available to rest. In the Chaco, the open horizon is pervasive in the landscape of everyday life. A few days after his arrival, a fire destroyed the place, and Valentín had to move elsewhere. He ended up in the Hotel de Inmigrantes (Immigrants Hotel), a place ruled by the National Migration Authority located in Retiro, adjacent to the Buenos Aires Port. It was different from the previous settlement; here he came into contact with people from all over the country and the world. However, he lived still worse than before. Indeed, it was so noisy that a chronic headache affected him. After about three months, he returned to the Chaco; an order from the authorities compelled all single men to leave the hotel. During his stay in the city, he had started to work in the port as a longshoreman. This allowed him to obtain the official working permit called *libreta del Puerto* (Port pass), which assured him a place in every call for jobs at the port. After the order to move, Valentín felt that it was time to go back to Las Palmas. In any case, he could return to work without major difficulties.

TO THE CHACO, BACK AND FORTH

Most of the *qom* settled in Buenos Aires return periodically to the Chaco. Disparate reasons motivate these sojourns—for instance, lack of work, illness, kin-related situations (marriage, divorce, or death), homesickness, or religious meetings. This produces a continuous demographic variation in all *qom* settlements in the Buenos Aires area and in Rosario.[11] Valentín was not an exception in this regard. During his first return to Las Palmas, he looked for *changuitas* (low-paid temporary jobs). Ultimately, he worked in Yataí with his stepfather in cane plantations and also making palm-wood sticks, all activities quite familiar to him. People were interested in Valentín's experiences in the big city. As had happened with himself before, he continued the strategic chain of socialization for travel proper to the *qom* by sharing his impressions with them. In this process, Valentín developed a comparative view about the Chaco and Buenos Aires. Indeed, they differed basically in the rhythm of work time. In the Chaco, one could continue to do nothing or work at a slow pace. On the other hand, in Buenos Aires, although there was much *trabajo*, one had to be always in motion. He felt the first return trip as a relief: "It seems that I was drowned; afterwards, when I returned to the Chaco, it seems that I could breathe." However, his early sense of despair in Buenos Aires gradually changed, and finally he became accustomed to and pleased by the speed and noise of urban life.

After his first return, a common pattern characterized Valentín's displacements. Since 1955 he has returned to Las Palmas several times, yet he has remained installed in Buenos Aires. From time to time, and after saving money for the bus ticket, he would take advantage of vacations or lack of work to return to Las Palmas. Generally speaking, once in Las Palmas, Valentín would almost always become caught up by the local way of life, meaning *cuestión de trabajo y de cacería* (work and hunting chores). The opposition of work and hunting is almost commonplace among the Argentine *qom*, a fact deeply rooted in their historical experience with white people. In this sense, it seems that *trabajo* refers to the labor introduced by whites (agriculture, salaried work), while *cacería* includes all those activities carried out since ancestral times (hunting, gathering, fishing, and the like). Moreover, it seems that *cacería* is less valued than *trabajo*. Anyway, Valentín appreciated very much his work in the Buenos Aires Port. Later his peculiar view of what constitutes "real" work is exemplified.

PARADOXICAL ADVICE

Once in Las Palmas, Valentín was asked by a friend named Antonino if he had a job in Buenos Aires, to which he replied positively. Valentín's answer encouraged Antonino to imitate his own sojourn; Antonino arranged everything to go to Buenos Aires. After a more or less successful period there, he returned to Las Palmas and wanted to bring back his younger brother

Marcelo, a hard worker and good soccer player. Before the trip, Antonino, who seemed sharper and more seasoned after the urban experience, gave some advice to his brother.[12] He told him, "Look, if you go to Buenos Aires with me, come with me, yes, but I can assure you that if we get there, you have to make acquaintances among *gente criolla* (creole people), because if you stay with Toba people you're gonna be always fooling around. Get smart a bit."

When Marcelo arrived in Buenos Aires, he followed his brother's advice. Later, one day Antonino found his brother drunk beside the Quilmes Club soccer field. Astounded by this scene, Antonino asked him, "What's going on with you, Marcelo?" "I'm here, watching soccer," he replied. "But look, why are you like that, drinking wine?" "Look, Antonino, didn't you tell me once, your advice was that I should look for criollo friends; so, I have many friends indeed, and they gave me this bottle!" Antonino stood still and sad, not knowing what to do next; his brother had obeyed his words of interethnic wisdom with unexpected consequences.

SETTLING IN THE SOUTH

It was not until Valentín's second trip to Buenos Aires in mid-1955 that he found a place to stay and organize his life. He was informed that a few *qom* families had moved from the Immigration Hotel to Dock Sud, a *villa miseria* right across the Avellaneda Bridge in Buenos Aires Province. Between 1955 and 1960 he lived there as a guest with different *qom* acquaintances. Finally, in 1960 he was able to buy a small house that had belonged to a *qoml'ek* who moved to Formosa. Valentín remained there until 1968, when he moved to Ezpeleta. Toward 1967 Valentín's younger brother Joel and his mother and stepfather left Las Palmas due to economic problems and joined him in Dock Sud.[13] At the time, Valentín lived together with a Formosan *qomlashi* (Toba woman) from Misión Laishí, but they were not getting along very well.[14] For that reason, shortly after their arrival, Valentín's relatives moved next door to avoid increasing familial tensions.

ORGANIZATION, ACTIVISM, AND RELOCATION

Life in Dock Sud was rather trying due to family problems and also because of a projected highway that would seize the whole place. In every sense, it was a precarious lodging. Things got worse in 1967 when some fliers started to circulate stating that if the settlement was not emptied within forty-eight hours, it would be burned by the local police. A year before, in June 1966, a military coup had ousted the democratic administration of the Radical party president Arturo Illia. For this reason, a systematic policy of cleansing the *villas miserias* and other places occupied by grassroots people was carried out. Also, political activities as well as public demonstrations were forbidden. In this context, the efforts of Valentín and his neighbors to vindicate their rights are remarkable.

Facing what appeared to be a bleak future, Valentín decided to share his concerns with other neighbors. Gradually, more and more people got involved, and a collective sense of commitment toward their settlement's fate emerged. In Valentín's words, "We started to get organized." Valentín was the only *qoml'ek* working for the cause; in this context, the ethnic variable was invisible to him. As he asserted, "I was thinking about the right to human dignity, just defending the human being."

As a consequence of this movement, a local *comisión* (committee) was created. It had to contact institutions and people who could help it to stop the forced resettlement. The committee turned out to be quite efficient; it got in touch not only with other *villas miserias* with similar problems, but also with civil and student associations that supported their claims. In this regard, Valentín was an active voice, and his ideas were very much appreciated. The committee's momentum peaked on the same day it visited the working-class-oriented newspaper *Crónica*, the General Labor Confederation (CGT), and the Ministry of Social Welfare. After tough negotiations, the latter produced a document that paralyzed the relocation and awarded enough time to settle the housing problem. That very day, in spite of the official prohibition to gather in public spaces, the excited and happy crowd rallied through Plaza de Mayo crying,[15] "We demand worthy housing!" and also, "Down with the military!" Curiously, Valentín is ignorant of how he did all this; he was not aware of his political role in Dock Sud or in the whole protest process. He did not perceive himself as an activist at all; on the contrary, he felt unable to become a leader. However, it is his thought that the situation compelled him to act as such. Once the events ended happily, the community organized an *asado* (barbecue) to celebrate, and it especially invited him. Unfortunately, due to problems with his wife, he could not be part of it.

Authorities had promised to stop the move until they could find an appropriate place elsewhere through a plan of low-cost housing. This materialized one year later. In 1968 the community received a notice that some *viviendas precarias* (inexpensive houses) had been built in Ezpeleta, a place about twenty kilometers south. Ultimately, Valentín's family and other *qom* and *doqshi* neighbors went to Ezpeleta. Ironically, the army provided soldiers and trucks to assist the relocation. The new place had small brick houses. Once there, Valentín chose a low profile regarding community matters to counterbalance his earlier public exposure. In fact, for him it would be fine living there as if he never existed. Additionally, he felt it necessary that nobody should find out that he was one of those who promoted, as "involuntarily" as it might be, the Dock Sud "uprising."

Political winds changed once again in Argentina, and Perón returned to power in 1973 after democratic elections. Among other things, social policies were activated; housing for grassroots inhabitants was a key governmental agenda. In this context, the administrator of Ezpeleta told the people that again, an "order" from authorities suggested that all who wanted to live in building-type apartments would have to move to Ciudadela, west of Buenos Aires City in the province. Valentín's new two-bedroom apartment was pretty comfortable and had enough room for his family. Because he recalled the bad experience with his ex-wife, the apartment's legal title was granted to his brother, mother, and stepfather. Right before leaving Dock Sud, Valentín had given away his house to his ex-wife; only after this did he feel confident that she would not bother him again. He wanted to own nothing; the future did not bother him. Doubtless, he was modestly confident that some blessing would appear.[16]

A WORKER'S MEMORIES

According to Valentín, a good job always implied much physical activity. As soon as he arrived in Buenos Aires, he started to wander through the port's docks. There he found the work he appreciated most, carrying bags on his shoulders, which he did almost continuously from 1955 until 1982. However, during times of low demand, he performed several other kinds of chores, becoming acquainted also with a rich typology of employers and the cold logic of capitalist entrepreneurship. Moreover, his work history is unstable, displaying almost a "nomadic" character. Inevitably, after a while he would eventually quit any job he was performing. In any case, fixed jobs were definitely not for him.[17]

Trench Digger

While Valentín was still in Dock Sud, he worked at trench digging. Pay depended upon the meters dug, so it was important to keep an accurate record. Unluckily, on many occasions the boss would arbitrarily reduce the meters in order to pay less. One day when Valentín was digging in Florida Street, a famous pedestrian street in downtown Buenos Aires, his pick hit an electric wire. As a consequence of the shock, he lost his grip, and the pick flew through the air and hit his feet. Because of the injuries, his convalescence lasted two months. At the time, Valentín had dug twenty-five meters, so once he recovered, he went to the employer's office to receive his payment. The boss treated him with irony and sarcasm, refusing to pay him what he deserved. After an unpleasant give-and-take, Valentín exploded, "Look, sir, forgive me, because it seems that you don't have time, I'm out of here. That money that I've earned is no longer mine, it's yours, you need it, you take it, it's yours!" Ironically, a few months later the boss, driving an expensive brand-new car, got stuck at a railroad crossing and was crushed by a train. Due to the injuries received, the man died.

Fancy Factory

Another time, Valentín worked in a textile factory stocking packages of fabric. It was an occupation that required neatness. Having everything well organized and clean, with paid coffee and lunch breaks, made him feel somehow uncomfortable. Similarly, his working clothes, a nice suit with tie, appeared too fancy for a *choGodaq* (poor person) like him.[18] He felt almost out of place there, in spite of being highly appreciated by fellow workmen and employers. Furthermore, Valentín wanted to be like a companion who used a little pencil to write down everything—calm and patient. He tried to be like him, but the attempt was futile; this kind of calmness and patience was not his way. He thought, "I can't stand being regularly dressed like this, surrounded by papers." Finally, against the employers' will, Valentín quit.

Bricklayer

Work in the textile factory had another handicap; it was indoors. Valentín loved to work in open spaces, feeling the sun and wind. This problem seemed to be eliminated when he was offered a job as an assistant bricklayer. He was happy working outdoors with the rest of the people. The work was smooth and light. However, he got tired of it; he did not know what he really wanted. Again, he quit and continued working in the port.

REDISCOVERING INDIANNESS

The Cause

When Valentín arrived in Buenos Aires, he was sure about his identity as a *qoml'ek*, but it was more an inner feeling than a public and militant attitude. Things started to change when Eulogio Frites showed up in Ezpeleta in 1970. Frites was a lawyer of Indian descent from Jujuy Province, one of the people usually known as *collas*.[19] They had met in 1954 at the Immigrants Hotel. At the time, Frites assisted a Mapuche leader of an official agency of Indian affairs. Valentín hardly understood Frites's interests because he was only thinking then about *trabajo*; activism regarding Indian rights appeared to him to be mere white politics.

The second meeting found Valentín older and more experienced in interethnic matters. Indeed, he agreed with Frites in valuing the Indian way of thought and the historical claims for land, education, and health, always overlooked by national authorities. He was invited to join a group of indigenous people to discuss the Indian situation nationally. Gradually, Valentín's commitment to Indianness strengthened, but it was restricted to what he considered a true Indian philosophy, colliding sometimes with his fellows' more white-styled activism. Ultimately, this group founded the Argentine Republic Indian Association (AIRA), whose Executive Committee Valentín joined from 1976 to 1980.

Indian Words in Canada

In 1975 Valentín traveled to Vancouver, Canada, with the Argentine delegation to the First World Conference of Indigenous Peoples. After an exhausting air trip, he attended a whole week of sessions discussing the situation of indigenous peoples across the world. On one occasion he was invited to give a speech. His message commented on the Indian situation in Argentina. More or less, he said, "As a Toba from Argentina, the only thing I can say is that we don't have lands, we don't have a place. All the brothers are marginalized; in some places they inhabit distant mountains around the country, stating that we're owners of these lands, but, on the other hand, it seems that we're not. What I just see is that they live far apart. . . . We don't have lands whatsoever. There are few brothers that are becoming politicized . . . but unfortunately they lack the consciousness of what the Indian is." He was congratulated for his words, which sounded very clear, "quite Indian" for them. Communicating through interpreters, Valentín discovered that he could relate to many fellow Indians who were agreeing with what he felt was the Indian way of speaking, posing problems, and coping with the current world. Though Valentín was away from home, he sensed that a general framework was shared by them all—a common heritage beyond particular differences.

Drums of Identity

During the conference's closing day, an Indian celebration was organized. A beating drum captivated the attendees' interest. People sang wordless songs and danced, following the drum's loud cadence. Valentín was fascinated by this scenario and joined in with deep joy. For him, these expressions were exactly like the *qom* way. People seemed to be guided by the waves of sound as the Toba are; they inspire in them complex, braided feelings. Later, everybody sat in a big circle, following the everlasting round model of sun, moon, and life. Then the pipe of peace was lighted and shared by all; embracing their prayer, they hoped that the smoke could reach God's heavenly abode. Due to lack of practice, Valentín could not sit cross-legged; many smiled at him, and so did he. No matter, he remained kneeling, enjoying the moment.

PRESENCES

The Dome

During a working day at the port, a crane was maneuvering with seven iron girders. By chance, Valentín was standing close by. Suddenly, an abrupt maneuver dangerously stretched the steel cables that tightened the girders. Consequently, they started to fall over Valentín's head. Instantly, he stared at them waiting for the smash, but to his surprise a sort of transparent, glassy "dome" appeared between him and the falling objects. Instead of hitting him, the girders crashed on the dome and fell to the ground. Still impressed by his "luck," he cried, "Gloria a Dios" (Glory to God); certainly he had a hunch that a divine presence would protect him, as had happened before.[20] On the other hand, and from a different hermeneutical locus, his work buddies teased him, "Hey, Moreno, what a tough head you have!"

The Smoker

Valentín was returning to Dock Sud from work at dusk. He had been walking along an abandoned railroad. Just before entering his house, he looked aside and detected a human figure over a set of bulrush plants beside the railroad. What attracted Valentín's attention was that the individual remained standing in the air. As he stared at him, he could see through him; the figure seemed sort of translucent. Wearing a white shirt and well combed, he looked like a young refined gentleman. He was blond and smoking; the smoke clouds produced by his cigarette could be seen clearly. Valentín began to pray and asked the man, "Why are you standing here, what do you ask for, what problems do you have?" "I'm looking at you and I feel pity on you." Afterwards, Valentín continued his walk home, and as he passed closer to the individual, he started to shiver from top to bottom. Nevertheless, an epistemological doubt assaulted him: was it true or not? He had to test what happened. For this reason, he marked the place to find it again later.

The next Sunday, shovel in hand, Valentín returned to the bulrush plants and began to dig on the wet surface. At some point the shovel hit a hard object; the digging continued by hand. There were human bones underneath! Valentín could grasp two arm bones and a skull. Doubtless, they belonged to the mysterious smoker. That was enough for him to clear away the shades of doubt. From there on he was sure about what he had seen, despite others' incredulity. Yes, nobody could deprive him of that. This occurred in 1966.

Dreaming Furniture

Once in December 1987 I went to Ciudadela to arrange a class schedule on Toba language with Valentín at the National Institute of Anthropology.[21] While we chatted about many topics, I raised an issue that had been puzzling me for a while. A police station close to my home had a clothing shop next door. I speculated whether these clothes could have belonged to people arrested by the police. In *qom* terms, I thought it possible that these clothes could keep their users' *lk'i*. This term refers to a sort of "soul-image" possessed by all beings and objects. Valentín understood clearly my question and answered, "Yes, indeed," expanding the point with a firsthand experience. After his retirement as a longshoreman in 1982, Valentín worked as a garbage collector in the Ciudadela building complex. The administrator had decided to clean his office and instructed Valentín to do this task. At the end, he gave him an old small stool that had been stored there for a long time. Valentín accepted it happily and put it in his bedroom as a night table. His apartment lacked electricity because he could no longer afford the bills. Thus he started to use candles to light the place. The stool seemed to fulfill perfectly its task. However, the very first night he dreamed a lot; a series of bad dreams bothered him. He dreamed about "strong things, people knocking each other, bleeding and crawling." He was deeply worried about his family's fate, and throughout the night he awoke many times. In the morning he was sure that the stool had something to do with his dreaming. Maybe it had been used by beaten or tortured people. Perhaps its owner had been involved in the guerrilla movements of the 1970s. The violence sensed by him could have had connections with that period.

Valentín asserted that Toba shamans "work" at night; through their nocturnal wanderings in dreams, they know what is going on about illness, for example. "I don't know if I'm half *pi'ioGonaq*, but they work that way!"[22] Finally, because he could not stand another night beside the stool, he threw it away into the garbage.

Further Advice: A Different Night in Ciudadela

Valentín has been my professor of the Toba language since 1980. Usually we gather either at his home or at mine to talk about his native tongue. Once we arranged a meeting in Ciudadela. As I was delayed at work, I arrived there at approximately 9:30 P.M. Fatigued by the run, I knocked at his door and he opened it a little bit, amazed by my presence. We sat together with his family and relatives who had arrived from the Chaco, engaging in friendly conversation. I felt that Valentín was embarrassed by my presence. During a conversation about differences in customs and behavior between the city people and Toba from the Chaco, he told me that in the Chaco nobody arrives as late as I had to visit friends or relatives, because everybody is at home resting or having meals. I finally understood my "mistake," bad timing, but not all its consequences. In addition, he continued to explain how elders taught the young proper behavior during day and night. He mentioned that there was *nqataGako* (advice) that dealt with these issues and began to relate it with unusual conviction. I was enjoying his performance, but at the same time I regretted lacking a tape recorder to preserve this wisdom within a natural setting.

Before I left, we arranged a new meeting to record, unfortunately out of context, the new advice. We met at my home, but now his discourse lacked the intense atmosphere of the previous meeting. Valentín told me a series of teachings about the difference between day and night. He commented that when I had arrived late at his home, he had been a little upset because he had thought that I should not arrive so late. In fact, he told me that he had actually doubted that I was the "real" Pablo, but had thought rather that I was the nonhuman (*jaqa'a*) Pablo.[23]

Indeed, as the teachings indicated, night is the cosmic realm of *jaqa'a* beings; correspondingly, day is the humans' abode. My tardy presence in Ciudadela implied a taxonomical problem for Valentín; clearly, I was in the wrong place at the wrong time. Valentín would misidentify me because I had infringed on key categories that order his social world. Once I had trespassed, my "presence" there had to be classified somehow; my only place could be as an existential "other." Fortunately, the "disorder" was repaired, and I recovered my human status again.

CRAFTSMANSHIP AND ETHNIC MEMORY

Before going to Buenos Aires, Valentín had observed in Las Palmas many *qom* making handicrafts. At the time, he lacked the intention to become a craftsman himself, but he learned how to make small clay animals and do strip weaving. However, once he was in Ciudadela, as time passed, he changed his mind and eventually planned to dedicate himself, at least partially, to selling handicrafts. An extra income was needed, and selling fit perfectly with his expectations. In the early 1980s, with the help of his wife María, he started to make birds and other animals to be sold locally, and sometimes in the Casa del Chaco (the official representative of the Chaco Province in Buenos Aires).

Toba handicrafts mostly include clay animal figures, decorated plates and teapots, masks, and basketry. Generally, they are not "traditional," but market-oriented objects. However, many painting techniques as well as design patterns are rooted in ancestral ways of representation displayed in archaeological pottery, string figures, and oral lore. In any case, it does not matter whether they are "Indian" or not; the fact that they are made by the Toba guarantees a certain quota of indigenousness symbolically relevant for *do-qshi* standards. Furthermore, as commodities, they are an important, if not the only, source of income for many *qom* in the Chaco and Buenos Aires.

On one occasion, a linguist friend of Valentín's was invited to talk about Indians at her children's school. Instead of going herself, she suggested that they invite Valentín. He went there and enjoyed the contact with pupils and teachers. In addition, many people bought his handicrafts. The idea of "talking culture" and selling handicrafts emerged there. After that, his work as a craftsman began to expand to other schools. In fact, while Valentín gave talks, his wife María arranged the craft exhibitions. The students were astonished to see and hear a "real Indian" in Buenos Aires. Argentine history had erased the Indian component from national identity; for that reason, the bodily presence of a Chaco Indian there was definitely moving. In turn, Valentín was pleased by their inquiries and fresh curiosity. It was a context for sharing a wisdom undervalued by whites, a true space for cultural inter-change. In addition, and no less important, he made good sales.

Due to this new endeavor, Valentín got in touch with other *qom* craftsmen living in Buenos Aires who were looking for housing in Ciudadela. He be-came especially acquainted with a young man named Pedro who asked him about his life in Buenos Aires and *qom* lore.[24] Valentín shared his *lkwen-nataGak* (thinking) with Pedro, who found it very enriching. In this context, Valentín illustrated for him, with an advice-type tone, his personal profile. "Look, Pedro, I've been living here for years, here in Buenos Aires, but my custom is as if I lived in the Chaco. I'm not still, I have nothing; thus I don't know how you think. It seems that you are a little disoriented, confounded, but from my viewpoint I'm not. So, if you want to think about what I've been explaining to you, well, think about it pretty well." He also com-mented about shamans, the past, and handicrafts; in short, about the *qom* way of life.

Ultimately, Pedro replied, "Look Moreno, your idea, your thinking seems to me pretty OK. Our youth need this [wisdom] in order to remain being themselves." Subsequently, they formed a committee to organize the group as a work cooperative, developed a circuit for different craft exhibitions and fairs, and committed themselves to "teaching ethnicity" in schools. Being the senior member, Valentín was the authorized voice to talk about *qom* histo-ries, an undertaking he enjoyed the most.

LAST MOVE

As a consequence of the lectures in schools, a network of teachers inter-ested in Indian issues emerged. When questioned about life in the Chaco, Valentín and his companions would depict the list of shortcomings affecting them: land, rights, education, health, and work opportunities. The teachers were shocked by this panorama and began to contact social workers, reli-gious institutions, and nongovernmental organizations (NGOs). They wanted to redress this state of affairs by providing support to the *qom* co-operative, even though the latter never made such a request. Thus, advised by these *doqshi*, members of the cooperative were invited to meet politicians and other authorities in order to present projects to palliate their needs. Per-sonally, Valentín had no plans to move anywhere, but Pedro and the other young men seemed more encouraged to undertake a "struggle for land" in Buenos Aires.

Word about the *qom* situation spread fast through institutions of social welfare, and ultimately, a Catholic bishop found an unoccupied site for them in Derqui, forty-five kilometers northwest of Buenos Aires. Two NGOs ad-vised the *qom* in the process of receiving the land and arranging a plan of self-constructed housing. Houses were designed after consulting *qom* view-points; materials would be provided by a Buenos Aires province housing agency and labor by the *qom* themselves. By January 1995 all the paper-work was set for the move.

The *qom* were eager to become installed there because life in the Ciudadela complex, sadly and ironically known as *Fuerte Apache* (Fort Apache) for its violence, had been deteriorating. Poverty, unemployment, and marginality had turned a low-income neighborhood into a dangerous place to stay. The historical irony ended when all the *qom* living there, and in other places as well, relocated to the two hectares of open field granted to them at Derqui.[25]

A new *qom* "community" was established, gathering together people from disparate places of the Chaco and Formosa. They are currently going through a hard time in the quest for unity. Problems with the settlement's committee are a case in point. In this regard, whites have played a key role in shaping this new "imagined community" (see Anderson 1983), which could hardly have existed otherwise.

THE CHURCH

After some time in Derqui, people wanted to organize a church there. However, this was not an easy task because almost all belonged to different denominations. It seemed that the only solution was to organize a new church locally. But given the fact that all non-Catholic churches need a legal permit to function, the so-called *fichero de culto*, an eventual indigenous church would have to apply for its own.[26] This procedure involved much paperwork.

Among the Toba, there are several "indigenous churches" that have arisen since the mid-1940s in the Chaco and Formosa provinces. They mixed elements of shamanism with Pentecostal Christianity, producing a novel religious and ritual framework called *el Evangelio* (the gospel) by the Toba. In terms of hierarchy and organization, the only 100 percent Toba church is the Iglesia Evangélica Unida (IEU, or United Evangelical Church), which has officially functioned since 1958, headquartered in Sáenz Peña (Chaco Province).[27]

Other institutions, like the Assembly of God, La Iglesia Cuadrangular (Foursquare Gospel Church), or the Pentecostal church, have indigenous pastors up to middle-rank levels; beyond that, control is held by whites, sometimes of foreign origin. The IEU is the most powerful religious institution among aborigines in the Chaco region. Indeed, it spread also among other peoples, like the Pilagá, Mocoví, and Mataco-Wichí. Currently it has also a small portion of white believers. Remnants of the first evangelical wave not absorbed later by the IEU still persist throughout the Chaco region and elsewhere. That is the case in Derqui, and particularly for Valentín. He had been baptized in Resistencia within a Pentecostal church named Vaya a la Biblia, an heir of the former Go Ye Mission, established by North American missionary John Lagar.[28] Valentín is still a member of this church today. In terms of beliefs and practices, he finds close links between Toba and biblical teachings. According to him, both emphasize love and respect between youngsters and elders; also, the power of God's Word functions like a shield to protect people from evil and disease, as shamanic prayer did.

In spite of the apparent hegemony of the IEU in the Chaco and also in Buenos Aires, Valentín and other people were faithful to their own church. Thus, because they felt themselves handicapped in obtaining the legal permit, I was asked for help to find out the requirements needed. Although I got the application forms and the required information, they informed me later that the entire process was suspended due to internal problems. Even though they obtained a temporary permit from the local police to carry out religious gatherings, organizing a church affects the community's power structure. Currently there is a conflict between the local committee and the "new church" supporters. A struggle for hegemony and control is under way; complex negotiations and dialogue will be required to settle the conflict. Valentín trusts God's power to illuminate the future steps. In the meantime, he depicted the state of affairs with a double sense of hope and hopelessness.

On the one hand, to avoid conflict, all the would-be pastors take turns in leading the religious services, which are still carried out in spite of everything. In this context, Valentín feels good because other candidates willingly let him take their own turn as pastors. On the other hand, everybody feels trapped by the paperwork required to achieve the *fichero*. The weight of paperwork as a key byproduct of the white order appears here in the administration of religion. As the popular saying goes, "God controls everything, but has his office in Buenos Aires." Moreover, any contact with him is obtained by filling out the right form.[29]

FINAL WORDS

Buenos Aires appeared as a new territory to be known and inhabited. More than 800 kilometers distant from the Chaco, it housed many *qom* who, disregarding distance, imagine an ubiquitous Chaco always available to bestow meaning on their lives.[30]

Migration did not imply breaking with their origins, but a true challenge to build a new life in tough conditions. Valentín's case showed how a Toba moved to a new place, supported by a network of relatives, acquaintances, and information that allowed him to find a place to live. Since then, while the Chaco is cherished, Buenos Aires has its own charm. *Trabajo*, Indianness, and religious life are key areas in Valentín's praxis. In addition, the struggle for people's rights was essential during his Dock Sud period. In this regard, the unmarked "Indian condition" for Valentín is surpassed by the more embracing category of humanness. Ethnicity is relevant under concrete circumstances, yet it always appears as deeply felt. Consciousness of an authentic Indian activism appeared when Valentín met Eulogio Frites in 1970. After that, a new dimension of struggle energized his life, but it was always framed by his perception of an Indian path of doing politics against the white way.

Some of the histories included unveiled a cosmology that does not split natural from supernatural in closed realms. Furthermore, it considers reality as a continuum within which God and other nonhuman beings can display their power. This has epistemological consequences for the interpretation of events. Indeed, life is understood in terms of blessing for the humble, a basic existential premise for Valentín and the *qom* generally. Indian activism allowed him to experience brotherhood with other Indian peoples of the world. The Canadian meeting reinforced Valentín's certainty of a true pan-Indian way of being and strengthened his views about ethnicity. The latter acquired a central place in his school lectures, where he discovered a novel space for cultural interchange.

The ethnic issue in Buenos Aires appears as a pending historical assignment for whites. It explains why teachers, social workers, and NGOs played a key role in the struggle for land in Buenos Aires. Within this context, the new settlement of Derqui is not only a concrete, material place to live but also a symbolic terrain in which white and *qom* imaginations cross each other. Furthermore, each regards the other as the object of utopian desires. On the one hand, Derquí allows whites to practice historical compensation and ethnic egalitarianism. On the other hand, it allows *qom* to arrange themselves as a "community," supported by a robust network of social help. Even though land is a blessing, organizing the Derqui community is difficult, and conflicts arise every now and then. In this regard, establishing the local indigenous church, an important institution to unify differences at other levels of social life, has not only religious but also political and legal consequences. These problems show the active role indigenous churches have in articulating interactions within the whole *qom* sociocultural network.[31]

Valentín is happy living in Derqui. He still possesses the apartment in Ciudadela. Sometimes his oldest son, José, takes care of it while working in the area. On other occasions, relatives who arrive from the Chaco are housed there temporarily. His other children live with him and go to a free Catholic school just across the street. He always plans to travel to Las Palmas to visit his brother Joel, who returned some years ago. Each time Valentín travels there, he receives much recognition for his famous heritage. Indeed, few individuals could be identified currently as direct relatives of a great leader. That is the case for him. His word is highly respected there. However, he lacks a leader's personality; he is more a philosopher who analyzes reality critically, but with a clear agenda. As he told me recently, more than anything else, he is concerned that his forefathers' wisdom not fall into oblivion, a prime directive that guides his life and questions the legitimacy of the official narrative about the Indian condition.

NOTES

1. This research was funded by the Argentine National Council for Scientific Research (CONICET). I am grateful to Valentín Moreno for his patience and generosity throughout many years of human interchange, to Jorge Wright for his linguistic assistance, to Matías Ruiz for his help with cartography, and to Elmer S. Miller for his useful comments on earlier drafts of this chapter.

2. In Argentina, *aborigine* is a common word to refer to the country's native inhabitants. The term "Indian" is a bit offensive. Nevertheless, in recent times, indigenous peoples have been vindicating their ethnicity through an active use of the word "Indian." Moreover, Indianness is a heritage to be supported against the hegemony of white culture of European origin.

3. In the Chaco Province, the barrios began in the late 1950s, in towns such as Sáenz Peña; later, they appeared in Castelli, Resistencia, and Las Palmas. In Formosa, Toba barrios began appearing in the 1970s, mainly in Lote 68 (close to Formosa City), El Colorado, and Clorinda.

4. Migrants to Rosario can be estimated at 2,000, while in Buenos Aires the numbers fluctuate between 800 and 1,200 individuals.

5. The presence of Indians in Buenos Aires is symbolically relevant for the non-Indian population. This issue is expanded throughout the text.

6. It is obvious that these questions were nurtured by a naive conception of what ethnic identity was: "one culture, one territory, one language." In this context, my field experience in Formosa and the Chaco had contributed to building a rather static view of aboriginal lifeways and identity. However, after fieldwork in Buenos Aires, this view changed radically (see Wright 1997, chap. 3).

7. Throughout this chapter, Valentín's recollections about past events in the Chaco and Buenos Aires are quoted. In some cases, they show reported speech, which appears as a useful linguistic device to retrieve past interactions. It is interesting also to note how Valentín evoked situations he experienced, as well as other cases reported to him by friends, for example, his Canadian speech, or the paradoxical advice given by Antonino to his brother.

8. The Las Palmas sugar mill was founded in 1882 by Irishmen Richard and Charles Hardy. During its highest point, it owned 104,000 hectares, formerly occupied by the nomadic *qom*. It mostly hired aborigines as a cheap labor force. The present-day towns of Las Palmas and Leonesa are rooted in the demographic and socioeconomic concentration produced by the mill. Due to low productivity, it was shut down in the early 1990s.

9. *NawoGa* supposes a close link between human behavior and animal species. During pregnancy, child infancy, and menstruation, the *qom* had a series of food taboos that forbade them to hunt and/or eat certain animals. In case they did so, children and relatives could be affected by diseases related to key features of the ingested animals. In short, during key moments of the vital life cycle, humans are most vulnerable; these taboos guide them as a moral code during this dangerous time to avoid being harmed by non-human owners of animal species.

10. This was a common practice until thirty years ago. A person could have as many "infection" names (*nawoGa lenaGat*) as cases in which he or she was infected.

11. A portrait of the *qom* installed in Rosario can be found in Griva and Stroppa (1983); Rodríguez (1992); and Bigot, Rodríguez, and Vázquez (1991, 1992).

12. *NqataGako* (advice) is moral information given by elders to youngsters that helps them to face the contingencies of life (see Wright 1991). Later, another example illustrates the features of this oral genre.

13. This is the basic pattern in *qom* migrations to the city. One member travels; after he or she is installed, other members start to arrive. This spatially bounded network leads to the emergence of *qom* settlements. Some of them can be sectors within a major place, like Dock Sud, Isla Maciel, or Ciudadela. Most migrants initially live in *villas miserias* until they move somewhere else, as in Valentín's case. There are few other cases of families that, after this first step, live individually elsewhere (see Mendoza 1989). Recently, *qom* barrios have appeared, like Derqui (discussed later) or La Plata (see Tamagno 1991, 1997). Up to now, both have had only Toba inhabitants.

14. Marriage within the ethnic group is more stressed. However, inter-ethnic couples are also found. Among the new generations born in Buenos Aires, this tendency is increasing.

15. The Plaza de Mayo is a key place in Argentine political history. During the May Revolution of 1810, people gathered there to claim freedom from the Spanish Crown. Ever since, important rallies supporting or rejecting authorities have been carried out there. The president's office, called Casa Rosada (Pink House), and the city hall are also located there.

16. This attitude is common among the *qom*. People expect to read "signs" in the universe that inform them about the course of events, for instance, dreams, weather conditions, animal behavior, and also body sensations. Generally speaking, any message is considered a blessing, a gift that can increase the vital power of humans (see Wright 1997). Because of his "believer" condition, Valentín trusted God's will. I return to this later.

17. While Valentín's work nomadism is an extreme, most *qom* migrants are hired in low-paid, temporary jobs (see Mendoza 1989 for more details).

18. In existential terms, the *qom* usually depict themselves as *choGodaq* vis-à-vis nonhuman powers, defined as *salliaGanek* (rich). However, in the inter-ethnic arena, mainly with whites of European descent, they use the same set of terms, placing the latter in the category of "rich." Interestingly, those who are "rich" (nonhumans or whites), precisely because of their affluence, are morally obliged to give away power and/or gifts to the "poor." This cosmological extrapolation is certainly rooted in the history of *qom-doqshi* relationships and the way capitalist production impacted upon a former economy of scarce goods.

19. *Collas* are Andean mestizo peoples inhabiting the former southern province of the Inca empire known as Collasuyu. They live in the Puna highlands of Salta and Jujuy provinces in northwestern Argentina.

20. Valentín had survived two critical situations in the Chaco in which he faced death. Reasons of space prevent my including these accounts here. What is meaningful is that the port episode was not new in Valentín's life, but was another case of the irruption of the numinous affecting the course of events.

21. As mentioned before, when I met Valentín in 1980, he had been hired as a native speaker for a seminar in descriptive linguistics. Thereafter, he collaborated in other courses at the university and other research centers. He liked this undertaking because he could show the richness of Toba language and oral lore. On the other hand, he found it too "light" in comparison to his work as a longshoreman.

22. When he was about ten years old, Valentín rejected shamanic power offered to him by the owner of the forest, *sancharol*. Afterwards, he converted to an evangelical church, but always felt a sort of ambiguity toward shamanism. In short, in spite of his unpretentious stance toward these issues, he feels that he possesses some kind of shamaniclike power. Toba churches have a critical "official" view about shamanism, identifying it as a devil-related practice. On the other hand, Valentín looks for a dialogue between both cosmologies. General information about Toba shamanism can be found in Miller (1975, 1979), Cordeu (1969–70), and Wright (1992a, 1997).

23. The term *jaqa'a* implies a basic ontological distinction for the Toba. *Jaqa'a* means "strange," "out of context," "different, "nonhuman"; it is opposed to *jaqaja*, which means "brother," "known," and "human."

24. Since I do not know the young man personally yet, his name was changed to preserve his privacy. On the other hand, due to our friendship, I felt confident enough to ask Valentín to use his name, to which he amenably agreed.

25. Ultimately, 32 families moved to the new place; the population involves about 120 individuals.

26. Roman Catholicism is the official worship in Argentina. In this sense, it is the unmarked religion, so to speak. Any other religious institution needs official authorization to operate.

27. However, from its origin, the IEU received assistance from North American Mennonite missionaries regarding paperwork and the edition of *Qad'aqtaxanax-anec, Nuestro Mensajero* (Our Messenger), a newsletter about IEU's activities. A detailed account of the emergence of Toba churches can be found in Miller (1967, 1979, 1995). Additional data about the IEU and the Cuadrangular churches is published in Wright (1988, 1990, and 1992b).

28. Miller (1979:116–131) gives a detailed account of the influence of John Lagar and other missionaries among the Toba.

29. The influence of writing as a cultural artifact on the Toba cannot be overestimated. Introduced by whites during the colonizing process, it acquired for the Toba a surplus value in terms of legitimacy vis-à-vis their former "oral condition." In this regard, the latter is felt as proof of cultural weakness. Paperwork, documentation, and identification are grouped in the same semantic field, called *los papeles* (paperwork).

30. The role of the Chaco in Buenos Aires is dramatically displayed regarding illness. When someone becomes sick with a disease white medicine cannot treat, he or she travels to the Chaco seeking a cure from a shaman and/or powerful church members.

31. This role is a fact little known to anthropological and sociological analyses that stress the "Christian side" of the churches' belief system or variables, such as "alienation," "secularization," and "politics." They neutralize the cultural dynamism of these institutions for the sake of an excessively Western-oriented conceptual background; see, for example, Fuscaldo (1982), Fort (1985), Santamaría (1990), Cordeu (1984), and Wright (1990).

REFERENCES

Anderson, Benedict. 1983. *Imagined Communities: Reflections on the Origin and Spread of Nationalism*. London and New York: Verso.

Bigot, Margot, G. B. Rodríguez, and H. Vázquez. 1991. Asentamientos Toba-*qom* en la ciudad de Rosario: Procesos étnicos identitarios. *América Indígena* 51(1): 217–251.

———. 1992. Los asentamientos tobas en la ciudad de Rosario. In *La Problemática Indígena*, ed. Juan Carlos Radovich and Alejandro O. Balazote, 81–100. Buenos Aires: Centro Editor de América Latina.

Cordeu, Edgardo J. 1969–70. Aproximación al horizonte mítico de los Tobas. *Runa* 12(1–2): 67–176.

———. 1984. Notas sobre la dinámica socio-religiosa Toba-Pilagá. *Suplemento Antropológico* 19(1): 187–236.

Fort, Mario. 1985. *Milenarismo y conflicto social: Los tobas.* Buenos Aires: Centro Editor de América Latina.

Fuscaldo, Liliana. 1982. *La relación de "propiedad" en el proceso de enfrentamiento social (de propiedad comunal directa a propiedad privada burguesa).* Cuadernos de Buenos Aires: Centro de Investigaciones en Ciencias Sociales (CICSO), Serie Estudios 42.

Griva, Edelmi, and María Cecilia Stroppa. 1983. *Yo, Montiel Romero, de raza Toba: Historia de vida de un indio Toba del Chaco Argentino.* Mexicali: Editorial Mar de Cortés.

Mendoza, Marcela. 1989. Estrategias adaptativas de migrantes tobas en el Gran Buenos Aires. *Acta Psiquiátrica y Psicológica de América Latina* 35(3–4): 139–44.

Miller, Elmer S. 1967. Pentecostalism among the Argentine Toba. Ph.D. diss., University of Pittsburgh.

———. 1975. Shamans, Power Symbols, and Change in Argentine Toba Culture. *American Ethnologist* 2(3): 477–496.

———. 1979. *Los Tobas Argentinos: Armonía y disonancia en una sociedad.* México City: Siglo XXI.

———. 1995. *Nurturing Doubt: From Mennonite Missionary to Anthropologist in the Argentine Chaco.* Urbana: University of Illinois Press.

Rodríguez, Graciela and Hector Vazquez. 1992. Historia, control social y representaciones simbólicas. De "lo rural" a "lo urbano" en dos grupos de familiás tobas migrantes. In Carlos E. Berbelgia (Coordinador), *Propuestas para una Antropología Argentina II*, pp. 87–95. Buenos Aires: Biblios.

Santamaría, Daniel. 1990. Pentecostalismo e identidad étnica. *Cristianismo y Sociedad* 28(3): 7–13.

Tamagno, Liliana. 1991. La cuestión indígena en Argentina y los censores de la indianidad. *América Indígena* 51(1): 123–52.

———. 1997. La construcción de la identidad étnica en un grupo indígena en la ciudad: Identidades y utopías. In *Globalización e identidad cultural*, comp. Rubens Bayardo and Mónica Lacarrieu, 183–198. Buenos Aires: Ediciones Ciccus.

Wright, Pablo G. 1988. Tradición y aculturación en una organización socio-religiosa Toba contemporánea. *Cristianismo y Sociedad* 26(1): 71–87.

———. 1990. Crisis, enfermedad, y poder en la Iglesia Cuadrangular Toba. *Cristianismo y Sociedad* 28(3): 15–37.

———. 1991. *NqataGako*: A Toba Oral Genre. Paper presented at the 90th Meeting of the American Anthropological Association, Chicago.

————. 1992a. Dream, Shamanism, and Power among the Toba of Formosa Province, Argentina. In *Portals of Power: Shamanism in South America*, ed. E. J. Matteson Langdon and Gerhard Baer, 149–172. Albuquerque: University of New Mexico Press.

————. 1992b. Toba Pentecostalism Revisited. *Social Compass* 39(3): 355–375.

————. 1997. "Being-in-the-Dream": Postcolonial Explorations in Toba Ontology. 2 vols. Ph.D. diss., Temple University.

Conclusion

Elmer S. Miller

Clearly the struggle for human rights, involving self-determination by way of access to natural resources that include land, is an ongoing dynamic reality for indigenous peoples of the Gran Chaco. It is a contention they share with natives not only in the Americas, but all over the world. While nation-states such as Argentina, Bolivia, and Paraguay are to be commended for their efforts to develop political and legal strategies that might redress justified concerns, it is far from clear that much can or will be done to restore the equilibrium with nature the people themselves desire and expect.

Certainly the United States provides no model for indigenous people seeking justice, since its record has been generally one to be deplored rather than followed. However, the voices of indigenous North Americans may have something to offer our friends in the Chaco. In the book entitled *American Indian Policy in the Twentieth Century* (Norman: University of Oklahoma Press, 1985), editor Vine Deloria, Jr., and other contributors call attention to issues of policy making and indigenous leadership involving both federal and state agencies that address many of the topics currently under discussion and debate in the Chaco.

These issues include leadership legitimated by community consensus rather than a simple majority based upon elections; how legitimate authority is perceived, where it is vested, and how it is exercised; techniques of co-optation used by both state and federal agencies to control Indian populations; the spiritual and physical well-being of the indigenous community at large; and strategies for engaging NGOs that aim to be of assistance. Certainly local traditions and ecology structure indigenous concerns in particular ways, but a forum for sharing common problems in the Americas has already been proposed and acted upon by indigenous peoples themselves in an effort to gain the justice they commonly seek.

Given that each author of this volume is an anthropologist, the question arises as to where we stand, or should stand, on the aspirations of the people whose experiences and causes we write. Traditionally, the discipline has defined its task primarily as one of calling attention to the struggle and seeking to be of assistance when called upon to do so. Several of the authors have chosen to become active advocaters for indigenous causes.

My personal position is that we can best be partners, not leaders, in this process. Every one of us carries national as well as disciplinary identity baggage that constrains our involvement with the people whose causes we seek to support. Our authority is limited among the people who are in a position to make their own cases for justice in ways that we cannot imagine. This is due not only to the limitations already noted, but also to the fact that however intense our interactions in the field of action may be, we are not and will never be insiders who share the collective history of a Chaco aborigine. Yet our personal involvement and writing can make a difference. We hope that this work will not only enlighten our readers, but also inspire them to action.

Index

About the Editor and Contributors

JAN-ÅKE ALVARSSON is a professor of anthropology at the University of Uppsala. He has published books, monographs, and articles that focus primarily on Mataco groups in the Chaco regions of Bolivia and Argentina.

JOSÉ BRAUNSTEIN is an anthropologist working with CONICET, the national research institute. For the past fifteen years he has been living and working in the Argentine Chaco among the Mataco-Wichí and Pilagá. He has published monographs and articles on indigenous Chaco peoples, with attention to ethnic classifications.

SILVIA MARÍA HIRSCH, an anthropologist living in Princeton, New Jersey, teaches at the College of New Jersey and Princeton University. Her research and writing involve Guaraní groups in western Bolivia and northern Argentina, with stress on indigenous political organizations.

STEPHEN W. KIDD is an anthropologist completing his dissertation at the University of St. Andrews, Scotland. He is Lecturer in Social Anthropology at the University of Edinburgh. His research work involves the Enxet (Lengua) peoples of Paraguay, political economy, and national indigenous policies.

MARCELA MENDOZA is an anthropologist living and teaching in Memphis, Tennessee. Her research and writing interests are the Western Toba groups in northwest Argentina, with attention to subsistence and family life in rural and urban settings.

ELMER S. MILLER is Emeritus Professor of Anthropology at Temple University. His focus has been on eastern groups of the Argentine Toba, with particular attention to socio-religious movements that have served to revitalize and expand self-awareness and determination.

PABLO G. WRIGHT is an anthropologist working with CONICET and teaching at the University of Buenos Aires. His primary research interests are Toba families in the eastern province of Formosa, especially shamanism as conceived and practiced over time and in diverse environmental settings.

ISBN 0-89789-532-0

EAN

9 780897 895323

90000>

HARDCOVER BAR CODE